T3-ALT-246

Ozette

Ozette

EXCAVATING A MAKAH WHALING VILLAGE

Ruth Kirk

UNIVERSITY OF WASHINGTON PRESS
Seattle and London

The publication of *Ozette* was made
possible in part by generous gifts from
Ruth and Alvin Eller and Robert Wack.

© 2015 by the University of Washington Press
Printed and bound in the United States of America
Design by Thomas Eykemans
Composed in Alegreya, typeface designed by Juan Pablo del Peral
18 17 16 15   5 4   3 2 1

All rights reserved. No part of this publication may be reproduced or
transmitted in any form or by any means, electronic or mechanical,
including photocopy, recording, or any information storage or retrieval
system, without permission in writing from the publisher.

UNIVERSITY OF WASHINGTON PRESS
www.washington.edu/uwpress

LIBRARY OF CONGRESS CATALOGING-IN-PUBLICATION DATA
Kirk, Ruth.
    Ozette : excavating a Makah whaling village / Ruth Kirk. — 1st edition.
        p.   cm.
    Includes bibliographical references and index.
    ISBN 978-0-295-99462-8 (pbk. : alk. paper)
1. Ozette Site (Wash.)   2. Makah Indians—Antiquities.   3. Excavations
(Archaeology)—Washington (State)   I. Title.   II. Title: Excavating a
Makah whaling village.
    E99.M19K575   2015
    979.7'99—dc23   2014025850

The paper used in this publication is acid-free and meets the minimum
requirements of American National Standard for Information Sciences—
Permanence of Paper for Printed Library Materials, ANSI Z39.48–1984. ∞

FRONTISPIECE: Geologist Roald Fryxell examines an excavation wall.
TITLE PAGE: Detail of an Ozette wooden artifact.

To "Doc" Dick Daugherty (1922–2014),
a visionary scholar with an entrepreneurial
spirit, who welcomed appropriate adventure
and lived life exceedingly well

CONTENTS

FOREWORD

Meredith Parker

"**P**ARTY AT OZETTE THIS WEEKEND. YOU GOING?" FOR SOMEONE TWENTY years of age that kind of invitation took mere seconds to process, and regardless of the location, the answer was always in the affirmative. There was to be a wedding of two of the staff members of Washington State University's Ozette Archaeological Project, and folks from Neah Bay were invited to both attend and play the traditional bone game, *slahal*. My backpack was at the ready, and I quickly filled it with the scant number of items required for a weekend jaunt down the curvy Hoko Road to Lake Ozette, the one-hour hike to Cape Alava, and what would turn out to be a life-changing weekend.

I grew up in Neah Bay on the Makah Reservation, where my extended family—my uncles, aunties, and dozens upon dozens of cousins—was led graciously and purposefully by our matriarch, my grandmother Meredith (Phillips) Parker. At different points in time we all lived under the same roof at her house, which is still located on the west end of the village, right across from the beach with the fantastic view of the harbor at Neah Bay, Wa adah Island, and, just across the strait, Vancouver Island. My grampa, Paul Parker Sr., had lost his life while out fishing in the Pacific Ocean, and Gram did an admirable job of carrying the heavy load of cultural responsibility for both of them.

Gatherings at my gram's house were always noisy affairs, with many people talking, babies making their presence known, coffee cups clacking against surfaces, and storytelling that predictably resulted in uproarious and continuous laughter as one story segued into the next. The room would quiet, though, when Gram would get serious and begin to tell the stories that were important for us to know. She would relate to us our family history, the roots and branches of our family tree, the connections formed hundreds of years ago between families and tribes, and the origins and meanings of the songs and dances handed down to us through the generations. She'd always tell the stories using the same words, gestures, pauses. "Oh boy," one of the young ones might mutter in an exasperated tone, "we've heard this one how many times?" But that is the way with our oral tradition, and we were all being taught the stories in the same way we now tell our own children and grandchildren, using the very same words, gestures, and pauses, and mimicking the twinkle in Gram's eye and her knowing smile.

I hadn't actually been to Ozette, though I'd heard plenty about it during the times I spent with Gram. During that inaugural hike to the site, I chose to walk apart from the rest of the chattering crowd, to reflect on those stories and really absorb the environment, with its lush, green vegetation, fresh forest smells, and the friendly sounds of birds and the light breeze that stirred the ancient boughs of the cedar trees. Grampa's father, Wilson Parker, was a whaler, and his photograph is displayed in the whaling exhibit at the museum at the Makah Cultural and Research Center in Neah Bay. Wilson's father, Tse kawilth, was a headman (chief) at Ozette and a signer of the Treaty of Neah Bay in 1855.

My gram's great-grandfather on her father's side, Ka oh badi, was also from Ozette. His wife, Tsi yac ta do, was the oldest daughter of Tse kawilth and a Klallam woman. On Gram's mother's side, her great-great-grandfather, A day ah tha wa, was a headman from Ozette. He took as his wife Tu tay a thlub from Kildonan on Vancouver Island, British Columbia. I have the great honor and privilege of carrying Gram's English name, and during a family naming potlatch in 1980 the name Tu tay a thlub was bestowed on me. It comes from my great-great-great-great-grandmother, who continues to strongly connect us to our Nu chah nulth relatives in Canada.

Our family ties to Ozette run deep and wide, and our family has many branches. As I made my way down the cedar-plank pathway, Gram's stories kept going through my head, and when I reached the beach I was moved nearly to tears. The beauty of the rocky coastline is expansive and impressive, but there was something else that stirred me. I didn't want to be moved by emotion at the time—I wanted to get to the gathering that lay just to the north—so I brushed my emotion off and quickened my pace.

The deep-rooted feeling within me would not be ignored, however; it grew louder and more persistent as the weekend of celebration went on. When it came time to hoist my pack and hit the trail back to the car, I knew that, before doing so, I had to ask about the possibility of working at Ozette. The project director, Jeff Mauger, was encouraging, and his words guaranteed my return to Ozette during the summer break from college classes.

I spent that first summer as a part of Washington State University's Archaeological Field School, painstakingly excavating in the upper layers of historic occupation, as well as in an area holding material from before the arrival of Euro-Americans. That area measured two meters by two meters and was rich with household items last touched by someone who was perhaps my own ancestor. I attended all the lectures, spoke the archaeological lingo, and was intrigued by student and staff interest in the village, the history, the people of Ozette, and the culture of Makah. My people! Gram had told us stories of her great-grandfather calling the people together by means of a carved bird set atop a pole. I wondered where it had stood. And I thought of the songs that had come to my ancestors at Ozette, and of how those songs have been kept alive and passed on at family gatherings by careful and exact oral traditions, by storytelling, singing, and dancing. At Ozette I had come home, and there was nowhere else in the world I wanted to be at that time.

Until I graduated from college, I returned every summer to work as manager of the Ozette Field Laboratory. Excavating—setting free objects that had not been seen for centuries—had been an amazing feeling. But being in the lab and gently washing, labeling, and cataloguing every single item gave me an even better view of what was happening, and having my hands touch those items somehow nourished the stirring feeling I had on first arriving at Ozette. After I graduated, my main goal was to move to the beach and participate more fully in the work at Ozette. I would call the little cedar-shake A-frame my home for the next two years. And even after that, I came back to work there summers, until the site was closed in 1981.

Dr. Richard Daugherty, or "Doc," as we fondly called him, was always busy as the project's principal investigator, overseeing reports and the analysis of discoveries and addressing issues of funding. But he was never too busy to spend time strategizing with the staff and volunteers, passing on worldly wisdom to the students and engaging in meaningful discussion with our Makah people, who were keenly interested in the "what next" of the project. From his very first walk along the beaches at Ozette through to his final visit to Neah Bay, Doc remained a loyal and trusted friend to our Makah people—and to me. I will forever be grateful for the way he encouraged me to take on greater responsibilities and to exhibit confidence, even when I didn't necessarily feel confident. Doc's mentorship influenced my educational pursuits, and later his guidance served as a factor in my career decisions.

Ruth Kirk was a frequent visitor to Ozette, and I was always impressed with the cameras, flashes, tripods, and gadgets she had on hand at all times, as well as with the crisp, clear photographs that resulted. I noticed the way in which she moved: quietly, appreciating all of earth's life in whatever form it appeared. And I observed how her images reflected back the respectful way she approached her photography. I set a goal to acquire my own thirty-five-millimeter camera and have continued to be inspired by her thoughtful work.

Ruth was observing and photographing and absorbing and writing. She was also visiting the women of my gram's generation in Neah Bay. To see her sharing a private moment with any one of the ladies was to see mutual respect and care for one another. During her last visit to Neah Bay, Ruth placed around my neck an olive-shell necklace that had been made years ago especially for her and placed around her neck by my gram. I shall forever treasure the memory of that moment and the simple necklace that signifies so powerfully the friendship through the years and the generations.

This book is long awaited, and there is no one better suited or trusted to tell this story than our friend Ruth Kirk. She was at Ozette, she was at Neah Bay, she was at our weddings, baby showers, and funerals. Her dear friend, and for seven years her husband, was Doc. They complemented one another perfectly and together have told the story of the tribe and the professor like no one else could possibly do. It is an important story, especially meaningful to our Makah people and our village of Ozette.

That offhand invitation to a party at Ozette forty years ago helped chart the course of my own life in a way that was meant to be: from field excavation, lab management, and curation of cultural materials, to language and photo archiving and research, and right up to my assuming my gram's spot on the board of trustees of the Makah Cultural and Research Center. The Ozette experience was for me powerful and persuasive, and brought with it the responsibility to maintain and carry out our Makah teachings in many forms—images, words, songs, touching of the heart, feeding of the spirit.

MEREDITH PARKER serves as the general manager of the Makahs, providing administrative, programmatic, and operational supervision for all tribal programs, activities, and business enterprises. She is also president of both the Makah Cultural and Research Center and the Potlatch Fund, among other volunteer activities. She has been featured in exhibits of her photographic works regionally, nationally, and internationally. Meredith coauthored a piece on Makah in the book *Listening to Our Ancestors: The Art of Native Life along the North Pacific Coast*, writes memoir, and contributed work to *Tribal Voices Echo*, an anthology edited by Tor Parker. She lives in Neah Bay, visits Ozette whenever possible, and has two sons and one beautiful, well-loved granddaughter.

PREFACE

I ONCE ASKED PROFESSOR RICHARD DAUGHERTY WHETHER HE PREFERRED excavating in the dust of eastern Washington's Snake River archaeological sites or the mud of coastal sites such as the prehistoric Makah whaling village of Ozette. Perhaps because he was born and raised in rainy Aberdeen, at the southwestern base of the Olympic Peninsula, his answer favored the mud.

Field archaeology is never simple. Neither is the process of obtaining enough funds to see a project through to a responsible conclusion, including scholarly analysis of the archaeological material that has come from the site. But as the Ozette project makes clear, the rewards can be great both scientifically and culturally. The story of these aspects stretches from two summers of preliminary excavation at Ozette to a subsequent, nonstop, eleven-year investigation of houses demolished and buried by mudflow. It is an account of a uniquely rich archaeological site and of scientists and tribal members working together, interweaving their perceptions and specialized knowledge. It is a chronicle of cultural legacy recorded academically by Washington State University archaeologists and now shared with the public at the world-class Makah Museum in Neah Bay.

My role as author and photographer stems from having lived on Washington's Olympic Peninsula and portrayed it in myriad magazine articles, Sunday newspaper supplements, and books such as *The Olympic Seashore, Exploring the Olympic Peninsula,* and *The Olympic Rain Forest.* I drove the back roads, hiked the trails and the wilderness coast, read the human history, interviewed first-generation descendants of homesteaders, and talked with tribal elders who remembered living at Ozette as children and who had family traditions of a mudflow that abruptly devastated part of the village. All of this made it only natural for me to look in on the archaeological project as soon as it got under way in 1966 and to continue looking in on it as often as possible for the next decade and a half.

At the time, the trail leading through the forest to the coast was notoriously muddy, and where it crossed Ahlstrom's Prairie the openness that native people had maintained by seasonal burning still prevailed. All this has changed. A board-walk now leads through the forest, and hemlock and cedar are invading the former prairie. Pioneering Lars Ahlstrom, who lived there alone from 1902 to 1958, would not recognize the land he claimed, nor would Ozette villagers who, for unknowable generations, had come to the prairie to pick bog blueberries and evergreen huckle-berries, dig edible and medicinal roots, and hunt deer. In large measure, the need for trail improvement was prompted by the thousands of people hiking out to tour the archaeological site, for it was a standard practice of archaeologist Daugherty to welcome the public to his excavations. He sought to stimulate awareness of the past and of how to read its record within the ground. He particularly welcomed journal-ists, and this led to our collaborating on several publications, most recently the book *Archaeology in Washington*, published in 2007 by the University of Washington Press.

In 1974 our book about Ozette for young readers, *Hunters of the Whale*, received the New York Academy of Sciences' Children's Book Award and the National Teachers Association's Outstanding Science Book award. At that time the Ozette excavation still had another seven years before its funds were exhausted and excavation ceased. This new book, *Ozette: Excavating a Makah Whaling Village*, tells the entire tale—the surprising preservation of wood and plant fiber within the earth, the use of water for excavating, the genuine partnership between the tribe and the archaeologists, including a hands-on opportunity for many high-school- and college-age Makahs to work at the site and in the preservation laboratory. The tale also highlights the ongo-ing value of the Ozette undertaking and its resultant archaeological collection.

Unfortunately, Doc, as his graduate students and Makah colleagues called him, was too ill to directly participate as this book inched from concept to actuality. How-ever, I had copious notes from countless conversations with him through the years, as well as access to his personal notes and to the camp's often refreshingly informal daily log. Additionally I read all the yearly Phase Reports detailing project expecta-tions and achievements, and all the research reports on which advanced degrees were based—nine PhD dissertations and ten master's theses from the one project. In addition I had taped interviews with Makah elders in the 1960s and '70s, and I am deeply grateful for their having shared with me some of their experiences, oral tra-ditions, and insights into cultural values. The generation who grew up with parents speaking Makah rather than English are gone now, but their descendants keep the old drumbeats alive, and the songs and dances and ceremonial names that link the past to the present and future.

For offering suggestions to strengthen this book from a Makah standpoint, I especially thank Janine Ledford, executive director of the Makah Cultural and Research Center; Meredith Parker, tribal general manager; Rebekah Monette, tribal historic preservation officer; and Dr. Ann Renker, linguist. Similarly, I thank Dr. Paul Gleeson and Dr. Dale Croes not only for information in regard to their own Ozette research but also for guidance on the book's overall gestation. They identified research material, read drafts, corrected misstatements, offered augmentation, and encouraged the stick-to-it aspect required for the transformation of a book from concept to printed—or electronic—pages. I also thank the many other Washington State University graduate students whose advanced degrees are based on Ozette research for helping with sections of the book that pertain to their particular expertise, and I am grateful indeed to archaeologist Dr. Sarah Campbell, who reviewed the entire manuscript and offered helpful comments. I also thank my son Wayne Kirk for patiently reading draft after draft and mentioning both possible additional content and improved wording.

Clearly, no book is the product of only the person whose name appears on the title page, and my deep appreciation goes to the University of Washington Press for genuine care at each of the many steps that go into shaping words and illustrations into a book. Throughout the last fifty years it has been my good fortune to have published books through the press, and although, of course, personnel there have changed in that time, expertise and enthusiasm have been unchanging, and I thank in retrospect the editors and designers of those past decades as well as those who shepherded this present book. Regan Huff, senior acquisitions editor, and Tim Zimmermann, assistant acquisitions editor, readied the raw material for scrutiny by copy editor Bonita Hurd. Senior designer Tom Eykemans (himself a former resident of the Olympic Peninsula) created the design and layout and drew the maps. Editing, design, and production manager Jacqueline Volin coordinated the various stages from manuscript to book. Hope Richardson did the proofreading. Thérèse Shere prepared the index. Above all, I salute my late husband, Professor Richard D. Daugherty, who initiated the Ozette project, guided it to fruition, and is remembered, beloved, and missed by many.

As the Makahs say, *Kle-ko, kle-ko,* to all.

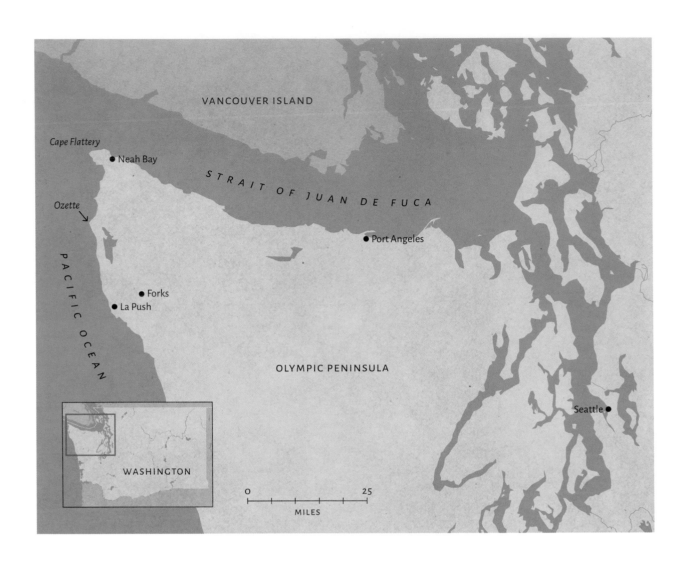

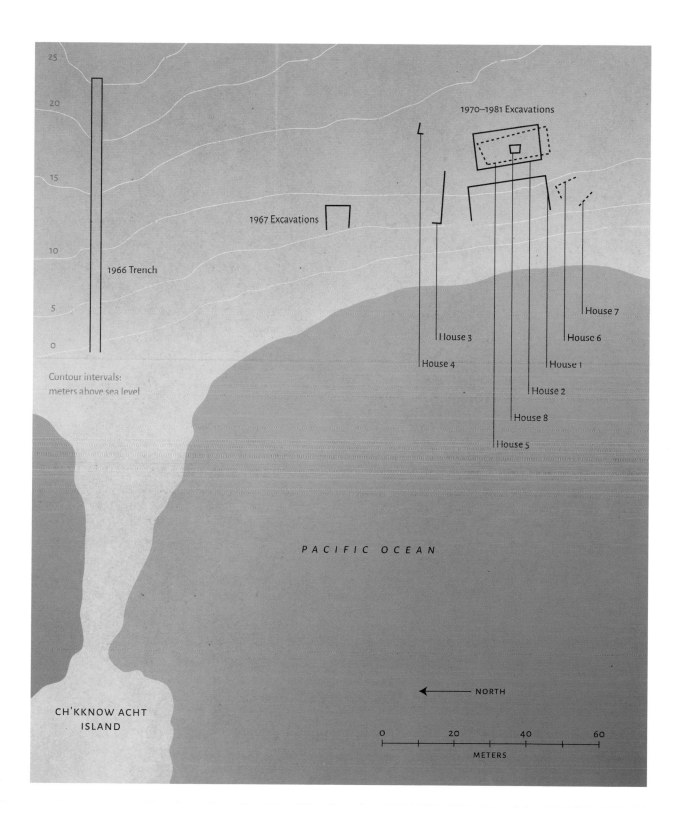

25

20

1970–1981 Excavations

15

1966 Trench

1967 Excavations

10

5

0

House 7

House 3

House 6

House 4

House 1

Contour intervals:
meters above sea level

House 2

House 8

House 5

PACIFIC OCEAN

← NORTH

CH'KKNOW ACHT
ISLAND

0   20   40   60

METERS

Ozette

The main Ozette village stretched
for about three-quarters of a mile
along the beach, connected to
Ch'kknow acht Island by a low-
tide sandspit.

Chapter One

Getting Started

PRELIMINARIES

THE YEAR WAS 1947. RICHARD DAUGHERTY, A STUDENT AT THE UNIVERSITY of Washington, was hiking the state's wilderness Pacific coast, recording archaeological sites. World War II had ended, and with it his service as a navy blimp pilot flying patrols on the lookout for submarines. He had returned to his studies and in connection with them was making this survey of more than two hundred miles of coastline, from the mouth of the Columbia River to Cape Flattery. Not far from the cape, he had reached Ozette, the site of a Makah whaling village. A broad terrace bordered the beach for a half mile or more, and on it the walls of a few houses lay fallen into the grass and nettles, along with rotten roof boards covered with moss. Families had lived there until the 1920s, when they moved to Neah Bay, sixteen miles north. The federal government had ordered their children to be in school, yet had provided none at Ozette. They had no choice but to move.

That exodus accounted for the end of the long human continuity at Ozette, but what were the beginnings? Midden—refuse—exposed in the sea bank edging the beach belonged to those earlier chapters. Lots of midden, and deep. Daugherty noted layer on layer of broken mussel and clam shells, whale bones, charcoal, and rocks cracked and split by the heat of a fire. This clearly was the premier site of the more than fifty he had recorded along the entire coast. He was *seeing* archaeological material that amounted to a cultural jigsaw puzzle belonging to the Makah people—and although he could not know it at the time, he was also *looking* at what eventually would provide the high point of his professional career.

Now the year was 1966. Daugherty had completed his PhD and joined the faculty at Washington State University, in Pullman. He had worked with other archae-

Tents provided shelter for the
1966 archaeology crew.

ologists in Egypt and Sudan, gathering evidence of the human past along the Nile
River before it would be lost owing to construction of the Aswan Dam. He had con-
sulted on Peace River archaeology in British Columbia and directed investigations
in eastern Washington along the Snake and Columbia Rivers. But he kept wanting
to get back to Ozette, and he found a way to do it. The National Science Foundation
approved funds for research, and Daugherty recruited thirty archaeology students
from across the United States and Canada to come and learn field techniques while
helping unlock the story of Ozette's past. The Makah Tribal Council had approved
the undertaking. Ed Claplanhoo, a young councilman at the time, was a graduate
of Washington State College (now University), and he knew Professor Daugherty.
Consequently the council asked his opinion of Daugherty's proposal. Years earlier
they had declined a University of Washington request for permission to excavate at
Ozette, but they could see merit in the current proposal as a way of strengthening the
tribe's tie to Ozette and they trusted Claplanhoo's assessment. The federal government was considering "surplusing" the land at Ozette as vacant and no longer eligible
for status as an Indian reservation. However, several Neah Bay elders had lived there
as children, and they cared deeply about those roots.

Hamilton Greene, one of the elders, remembered "a solid line of houses facing the
water, and canoes on the beach. My grandfather used to say that Ozette had been
a big village. The word he used to describe it means 'a whole bunch.' More [houses]
than you'd care to count." Daugherty's proposal seemed like a way to augment such

GETTING STARTED

The beach served as lunchroom.

memories with a new kind of knowledge. The tribe and the professor would work together.

The archaeology camp was set up just back from the beach, where a splashing creek furnished water for drinking and for icy showers. On days when it was not raining, the crew ate out on the beach, sitting on drift logs. On drizzly days, they gathered in a large, floorless tent designated as mess hall and classroom. A Coast Guard helicopter had brought in the big tent and smaller sleeping tents, a cookstove, groceries, shovels, surveyor's transits, and field notebooks and laboratory catalogs with blank pages to be filled with information day-by-day as the excavation progressed. It was a onetime delivery. From then on, supplies had to be backpacked four miles through the forest and along the beach or flown in by a small plane twenty-four miles from the logging town of Forks. Often it was too foggy for the plane to land, and, for the same reason, travel often was unsafe by boat from Neah Bay, sixteen miles north, or La Push, eighteen miles south.

By modern standards Ozette is isolated and remote, but it was quite the contrary during its long years as a village approached from the sea. Sixteen houses stood there in 1834, according to the report of three shipwrecked Japanese seamen who had drifted for more than a year across the Pacific Ocean before finally being washed ashore and captured by Ozette Indians. They were subsequently rescued by the Hudson's Bay Company and eventually taken to Macao, a trade center on the southeast coast of China. A half century later, the 1889 *Pacific Coast Pilot* also mentioned Ozette,

A trail through the forest leads from road's end to the beach.

with a reporter stating: "Passed close outside [Ozette] and had a fine view of it. The village has over 20 houses and is not bulkheaded to prevent the inroads of the sea."

There could scarcely have been a better setting for Northwest Coast human life. Several offshore islands and a wide rocky reef at the village doorstep broke the force of swells and incoming waves, thereby easing the landing of canoes. The reef, exposed at low tide, hosted year-round edibles such as mussels, clams, sea urchins, snails, chitons, limpets, crabs, and octopus. About twelve miles west, nutrient-rich water welled up from the edge of the continental shelf and concentrated the plankton; fish fed on the plankton, and fur seals fed on the fish. That abundance of food brought migrating seals closer to shore at Ozette than anywhere else along the entire coast from Northern California to Alaska. Sea lions hauled out on the rocky points and beaches of the islands. Kelp beds furnished ideal habitat for sea otters. Red snapper and lingcod—bottom fish—thrived close to the village. Halibut banks were a short paddle away, and salmon came to the Ozette River a little over a mile to the north. Red cedars in the forest behind the village supplied planks for houses and bark for baskets, and they also could be made into dugout canoes. Deer and elk roamed the forest, which was interspersed by treeless prairies where villagers could gather a variety of plant foods and medicines.

Archaeology is not a search for things; that would result only in accumulating objects. The actual goal is to study relationships between objects and the people who made and used them. Archaeology is piecing together what human life was like through the long years before there were written records. It entails knowing the plants, animals, geology, and soils of the past—and Washington State University had a range of such specialists within the Department of Anthropology. That was a big part of why the university received National Science Foundation funding for the project. Daugherty saw archaeology as interrelated with various academic specialties. At the time, that was a largely untested concept, but Daugherty believed in it enough to initiate a multidisciplinary studies program. Geologist Roald Fryxell was available to help direct the Ozette project and coordinate input from colleagues in other disciplines. Zoologist Carl Gustafson headed the advance crew that set up camp, and then he stayed on to identify bones from the excavations. He concentrated on mammal bones; others analyzed fish bones and shells.

Ecologist Rex Daubenmire investigated possible relationships between present vegetation and archaeological sites where buried organic material was affecting soil acidity. For example, if you looked where nettles were growing exuberantly, the chances were good that a shell midden was neutralizing the acid in the soil there. Plant pathologist Shirl Graham studied soil samples, checking whether it was a lack of oxygen, and therefore a lack of soil organisms, that created favorable preservation conditions or whether groundwater infused with something from the forest accounted for the preservation. Palynologist Cal Heusser had recently collected and

Sea lions hauled out on rocks offshore from Ozette, and fur seals came closer to shore there than anywhere else along their annual migration route.

identified pollen and seeds from various places and at various depths in the vicinity of Ozette, important because most plants need specific conditions in order to grow well, and therefore past vegetation can answer questions about past climate as well as about resources available for human use.

THE TRENCH

Daugherty and Fryxell decided to excavate a trench up a hillside with a conspicuous series of terraces. As brush was whacked out of the way, the men realized they were mistaken in their assumption that the terraces were leveled house sites. "In reality," Daugherty wrote in his field notes, "they are old beach terraces. This may prove extremely interesting in terms of early occupation."

Every shovelful of the lengthening and deepening trench had to be examined. When something was found, a description of it and its exact location had to be recorded, and the excavation walls had to be drawn to scale. By the middle of July the trench, two meters wide, reached more than forty meters up the slope. On one single day, students unearthed seventy-two artifacts, a discovery record. In fact, they had found so many that they joked they would be late for dinner because of all the notes to write up. Daugherty cautioned that the site was being destroyed as the digging progressed: it could never be put back together to allow a second look.

Notes mattered. Students worked as partners. One shoveled, skimming the deposits and tossing midden up onto a table, where a second student troweled through it watching for artifacts and bones and shells. When that shovelful was finished, a call of "Ready" would send up the next shovelful. Broken dishes and pieces of glass kept showing up in surface layers. So did rusted nails, part of an old-fashioned muzzle-loading rifle, and two beautiful china doll heads. These items belonged to the last years of the Ozette village. Lower layers dated from the centuries before contact with Euro-Americans. There the students found whalebone clubs, chisels and gouges and hammer stones, bone knives and stone knives, a clamshell still holding red pigment, bone fishhooks with stone shanks that acted as sinkers, simple net weights made of stone, a bone comb with a human face and a hole drilled through the forehead to accommodate a cord and permit wearing as a pendant. By the end of July more than two thousand items had been found, cleaned, inspected, numbered, and cataloged. By late August the count was more than four thousand artifacts, and the trench stretched seventy meters from today's beach to the uppermost terrace. Radiocarbon dating indicated that the midden was sixteen hundred years old. Yet the midden showed little variation through time, whether in faunal remains or in styles of stone, bone, and shell artifacts.

Gustafson identified bones representing 1,140 individual mammals, of which most, by far, were northern fur seal. Clearly, for century after century, seaworthy

Students excavated a trench seventy meters long, cross-sectioning deposits that date from recent years to about sixteen hundred years ago.

A bone comb a little over five centimeters long came from the trench, one artifact among a total of more than four thousand.

canoes and navigational skills had characterized life at Ozette. Fur seals must be hunted on the water; their time ashore is limited to a brief breeding period. Whale bones, too, pointed to human expertise afloat. Some were so big they hindered excavation; several ribs and jawbones actually spanned the trench from side to side. Students identified and photographed them in place. Then, so that digging could continue, they sawed them apart and cleared them out of the way. Sometimes a whale vertebra was handy to sit on, and for a while a scapula (shoulder blade) sticking out of the excavation wall happened to be at a perfect height for use as a table while writing up notes.

Fryxell described his work as staring at trench walls until they made sense. The deposits had built layer by layer. The problem was to read what they recorded. At the time, most archaeologists regarded middens as garbled trash heaps to be excavated at arbitrary levels, their stories thus deduced without much consideration of actual relationships and sequences. Daugherty and Fryxell thought differently. Every midden builds bit by bit regardless of how many human generations contribute to it. The record is there and can be discerned. Surface layers cross-sectioned by the trench held the roots of today's plants, and mixed in with them were rusted nails and broken dishes from recent houses. Immediately below might be twenty-five or thirty centimeters of broken clam and mussel shells, a whale rib or fur seal bones, fish vertebrae or red-brown sand and heat-cracked rock. Paper tags pinned to the trench walls marked where artifacts were found—and slugs, which commonly grow six to eight inches long in western Washington, persisted in eating the tags.

By examining excavation walls, geologist Roald Fryxell could trace layer upon layer of time at Ozette.

In places, Fryxell could pick out where a prehistoric house had stood. A thin layering of soil and sand and debris from the packed-earth floor still showed, as did postholes filled with sediments that differed from those of adjacent deposits. In the bottom of the trench was a hearth consisting, Fryxell wrote, "of jumbled fire-cracked rocks, charred shell and shell fragments, charred wood, seal bones, and pebbles with wood ash." It was topped by three meters of midden, a steady accumulation that perhaps took centuries to form. At least once there had been a stone seawall to help protect the village; a cross-section of it was exposed in the trench wall. All such features became pieces of the archaeological puzzle, along with the bones and artifacts. Nothing pointed to long periods without human occupation.

Students made scale drawings of trench walls, recording everything measuring two centimeters or more in size whether a rock, a shell, a bone, or an artifact. Actual samples of trench walls also became part of the record. The technique for obtaining them called for isolating a vertical column of the wall and soaking it with Vinylite resin. After letting that dry, students placed a board against the face and gingerly threaded strips of cloth behind the column to tie it onto the board. The column thus stabilized, they could lift it out with all layers intact. Soil science professors at Washington State University had developed the technique, and Fryxell adapted it to archaeology. Twenty such columns, called "monoliths," were taken from the trench walls. They formed a sort of library that could be studied in detail at any time. They augmented the drawings of trench walls.

An overall understanding of coast geology seemed to grow more complex as the summer went on. Yet deciphering the geology was the only way to know when the area first became suitable as a dwelling place for people. During the maximum stage of the last ice age, about fourteen thousand years ago, a glacier a half mile thick covered the northern Olympic Peninsula and extended out into what now is ocean. Along today's beach, scratches in bedrock record the tracks of rocks held at the bottom of yesterday's moving ice, and granite boulders brought from Canada by the glacier lie scattered, some of them as big as automobiles. Gravel, clay, and silt also rode the glacier and washed out as it melted. Offshore islands are capped with these sediments. Geologists agree on this basic part of the coast's past, but what happened after the ice age closed has been less easily understood. It seems clear that as the enormous weight of the glacier was released, the land slowly rose. But earthquakes have partly offset this rise by causing coastal subsidence. The rate of uplift is now believed to be about four meters in a thousand years, and that of subsidence, one and a half meters in a thousand years—a seesaw but with an overall rise. Fryxell checked the evidence. What today is beach must have been below water in the past. And what now are terraces back in the forest must once have been beaches. The highest terrace would be the oldest. It would be where to find the earliest human evidence—and the walls of the trench bore this out. Shell and bone there were almost entirely rotted and gone, as would be expected with the passage of a great length of time. A dark stain was about all that remained. Whatever tools of bone or shell the early Ozette people may have had were no longer present. They had rotted. So had wooden and fiber objects. Only stone was left.

UNUSUAL PRESERVATION

Summer 1966 ended. So did field school. But a small crew stayed on to test the extent of cultural deposits at the Ozette village site. Daugherty and his assistant, archaeology graduate student Harvey Rice, used an auger to sample a meter or so beneath the surface, and what they found led them to arrange for a trailer-mounted hydraulic coring machine to be flown in. The new rig was heavy and bothersome to drag along the terraces, but it allowed them to sample as much as six or seven meters below the surface. Midden in two cores was so well preserved it looked almost fresh. This was puzzling because midden at similar depths in the trench had decomposed. Studying the cores, Fryxell noticed that in places massive layers of clay capped layers of preserved midden. He even found wood, intriguing because its depth below the surface meant it was old, yet wood and plant fiber usually decay within a few years. They remain only if constantly dry, frozen, or wet.

Based on cores, Fryxell made additional tests south of the trench and found water-saturated clay deposits interbedded with midden that contained well-preserved plant material. Clearly, this called for investigation, but there was no time to do it. October had come. The field season was over. The cores and other samples were packed, ready for study back at the university, the tents taken down, the equipment gathered. The men waited on the beach for the small plane that would fly them away from Ozette. Cow parsnip plants lining the trench had grown head-high and turned brown. Winter rains had begun. Vees of geese were flying south.

Back at the university, classes began again and analysis of Ozette materials and records got under way. Daugherty worked on plans for additional Ozette field seasons and their resultant studies and on how to fund such an undertaking. Rice and other graduate students sorted artifacts. Fryxell prepared the monoliths and geological samples for permanent storage. He also combined individual scale drawings of the trench walls into a single rendition for each side of the trench. The result required two rolls of paper twenty feet long. Gustafson continued identifying bones from the excavation, a total by then of almost eighty thousand, both whole and fragmented. There were fifty-one thousand mammal bones and pieces of bones, not including whale bones; nineteen thousand fish bones and pieces; and

Roald Fryxell combined stratigraphic drawings of the entire trench. They showed deposits as little as two centimeters thick, along with stones and bones, hearths and postholes. These drawings formed the first detailed record of a Northwest Coast midden.

ten thousand bird bones and pieces. Just sorting them took six months, even with an assistant.

After that Gustafson traveled to Washington, D.C., to compare selected Ozette bones with those in collections at the Smithsonian Institution. Sometimes identification could be made by comparing size and shape, other times by how muscles or tendons had been attached, or by how joints fit together. With the fur seals, males could be distinguished from females by the size and shape of the teeth, and in the Ozette collection half of the male teeth from the trench excavation came from seals more than five years old. This indicated a major change in seal migration routes in the last few centuries. Males of that age are now a rarity south of Alaska, but earlier they must have belonged to a rookery near Ozette.

When summer came again, project staff members and a small crew of students hiked through the forest to the beach, ready to resume excavation. This time Daugherty and Fryxell wanted to test the top of a small, steep-sided island that is joined to the village beach by a low-tide sandspit. Judging by its character and position—and by ethnographic information—the island must have served as a lookout station from which to watch for spouting whales and the approaching canoes of guests or raiders, and also as a defendable retreat in case of attack. There, too, midden lay about three meters deep, the residue from countless basketsful of clams and fish and seal meat carried up the steep path to the top of the island. The deposits dated to as much as two thousand years ago.

Japanese coins may have washed onto the beach as flotsam or been taken in trade with other people along the coast.

Excavation plans also called for investigating an area where 1890s photographs showed a row of houses a little way south of the previous summer's trench. The work went smoothly and routinely, with items such as ceramics and glass recovered along with stone and bone tools, bits of clam shell and mussel shell, fish vertebrae and whale bones. Also found were parts of rusted rifles, small hand-rolled copper tubes, Japanese coins, a buttonhook, a knife blade hammered from part of an automobile spring, an awl or punch fashioned from a nail, and iron fittings from a ship, probably the storm-driven barque *Austria*, which wrecked on the reef fronting the village in 1887. Its anchor still lies among the rocks exposed at ebb tide.

A wet area of the sea bank drew special attention. It held rope twisted from cedar or spruce boughs, torn cedar-bark mats, and several baskets. All were well preserved; evidently they had lain constantly in wet muck, sealed off from air and thereby protected from the bacteria and fungi that ordinarily decompose wood and plant fiber. The previous summer Fryxell had noted indications of several mudflows along the slope above the sea bank and had marked them with stakes. Now he found the stakes were tilted; the slope still held soggy layers that at times switched from slowly oozing to rapidly flowing. This fit Makah oral traditions of a mudflow that swept into the village one night, knocking down houses and burying them. Everything those houses had held might still be there, the product of a catastrophe that suddenly stopped time.

Confirmation of this seemed to come from a test pit three meters deep that had been dug to see whether cultural material like that found along the sea bank was also present well back from the beach. As the pit deepened, water seeping in from an upslope aquifer began to soften its walls, threatening collapse. But just as Daugherty was about to call a halt to their exploration of the pit, one of the students felt his

Wet Sites

By definition, wet sites are anaerobic and therefore unsuitable for the fungi and bacteria that require oxygen and cause wood and plant fiber to decay. Bogs are one type of wet site. They are not uncommon along the Northwest Coast but have received little archaeological attention, and many are now disappearing owing to commercial use of their peat or to their conversion into ponds for wildlife. An exception to such loss is the Manis Mastodon archaeological site near Sequim on Washington's northern Olympic Peninsula. It dates to

Small Ozette trinket basket

13,800 years ago, the time when the last ice age was about to wane.

Sites with water constantly flowing underground from aquifers are another type of wet site. They may be situated along river channels; at estuaries, tidal flats, and sloughs; or at shell middens with springs or creeks; or may be buried and sealed beneath landslides or mudflows, as at Ozette. Their deposits hold items made of wood, bark, boughs, roots, and grass, which are all materials ordinarily quickly lost to decay. That loss is major, because 90 percent of the physical evidence of Northwest Coast culture was made of precisely those materials. The oldest such sites known so far are in the intertidal zone of British Columbia's Queen Charlotte Islands. Discoveries there include wooden wedges, basket fragments, braided cordage, and part of a gill net—humble items that establish a human presence dating as far back as 10,700 years ago.

In Washington, the Biederbost wet site along the Snoqualmie River northeast of Seattle was discovered in 1959. It established the potential value of such sites. First, a carved wooden bowl dating to two thousand years ago washed out of the riverbank during a flood. Then, water-polished stones appeared, typical of streambeds, yet *not* typical. They showed no chipping or other cultural modification but were girdled with willow withes that were held in place by strips of wild cherry bark. They were anchor stones. With them lay basketry fragments and cordage, all probably from fish weir operation. The preservation was both impressive and unexpected. Northwest Coast archaeologists were not seeking wet sites in the 1950s, nor were they trained in excavating them or caring for what they might yield. Ozette was a turning point.

In a wet area, students found remarkably well preserved basketry.

A remnant of a classic Northwest Coast pack basket is identifiable by the loops along the rim (*at right*), which permitted attachment of a tumpline. A similar remnant dating to three thousand years ago came from the nearby Hoko River wet site.

shovel hit something solid. He probed and found wood—a plank covered with a cedar-bark mat. Under it lay pieces of basketry and more planks, one of them ten centimeters thick, its edges as beautifully straight and squared as if cut by a modern saw. A few pieces of basketry and mat fragments could be removed from the pit but the plank extended into the midden beyond the pit wall and had to be left in place. Clearly, this must be where a house had once stood, and the clay blanketing the exposed planks must indicate that a mudflow had smashed the house and locked its ruin within the earth.

Also clearly, a proper job of excavating Ozette was going to take months, maybe even years, yet time for fieldwork was again running out. Classes at Washington State University would soon resume. Funds were nearly gone. Furthermore, urgent salvage archaeology in eastern Washington demanded the team's full attention. Construction of Lower Monumental Dam on the Snake River was threatening archaeological deposits at Marmes Rock Shelter—which had just been radiocarbon-dated to the close of the last ice age, about ten thousand years before the present (the date for the deposits has now been corrected to eleven thousand years B.P.). At the time, human remains there were the oldest known in the Western Hemisphere. Daugherty and Fryxell, Gustafson and Rice, needed to return to the Snake River. Ozette would have to wait.

Wooden carving found at Ozette.
Its head measures ten centimeters long, and the carving's total
length is forty-one centimeters.

Chapter Two

A Buried House

PHONE CALL FROM THE MAKAHS

THREE YEARS PASSED. THEN IN FEBRUARY 1970, DAUGHERTY RECEIVED A phone call urging him back to Ozette. The call came from Ed Claplanhoo, who by then chaired the tribal council. Storm waves driven high onto the beach were undercutting the sea bank at Ozette and it had slumped. Deep layers were exposed, and fishhooks of wood and bone, parts of inlaid boxes, and a canoe paddle had washed out and been carried off by hikers. Daugherty listened. From what Claplanhoo said, he would need to find financing, set up a camp, hire a crew, round up the necessary field equipment, and resume excavating at Ozette as soon as possible. But first he needed to see the situation for himself.

The drive to the coast from the university in Pullman meant traveling from the southeastern corner of the state to the northwestern corner; it took almost ten hours. Daugherty slept for what was left of the night at the head of the trail and at dawn hiked the familiar four miles to Ozette. Claplanhoo and a delegation of Makahs met him, and together they examined the slump. Banks along beaches everywhere give way as a normal part of erosion, and several sites mentioned in a 1917 report on the coast by Albert Reagan, a schoolteacher in La Push, were nowhere to be found thirty years later when Daugherty made his survey. They had been swept into the ocean.

The slumped bank at Ozette was about four meters high. Wild crab apple, elderberry, and sword ferns had slid with midden and mud and now formed a junglelike tangle. The men climbed in among the roots and limbs, sinking nearly to their boot tops in the ooze. Their eyes lit on the ends of planks sticking out and a basketry hat of the kind women had twined from cedar bark in the old days. There were bone points used for shooting birds, wooden halibut hooks, an empty cedar-bark sheath for a

Richard Daugherty (*left*) and Ed Claplanhoo assessed the sea-bank erosion caused by winter's storm-driven waves.

harpoon blade, baskets, and part of a carved wooden box. If this much was washing out, what more might remain? A major excavation was needed, and right away. The National Science Foundation had granted funds for the earlier work, but arranging financing through any foundation is a lengthy procedure. A research proposal must be submitted, evaluated by a panel of experts, and approved or rejected. There really was not enough time for such a formal procedure. Waves were continuing to batter the beach; cultural deposits were continuing to be lost.

Claplanhoo called a meeting of the council. Here was a chance, as he later expressed it, "to see some of the things our grandparents and great-grandparents have been telling about for years." The resumption of archaeology at Ozette would be a new way to perceive the roots of Makah culture. Tribal elders (in Neah Bay, often called senior citizens) still told the old stories, reminisced about sealing and fishing—and even whaling—by canoe. They taught young people their family songs and dances and among themselves spoke Makah. Women asked husbands and sons to help with the heavy work of peeling bark from cedar trees so that they could weave baskets, and each August the Makahs invited tribes from Washington and British Columbia to come to Neah Bay for canoe racing, feasting, and dancing. The culture was still alive, and renewed archaeology would open a unique window onto ancestral life before

A BURIED HOUSE

Pollen taken from bogs near Ozette indicates that red cedar trees have been present for the last four thousand years. Stripping bark does not kill the tree so long as a quarter of it remains intact.

the time of written records and family memories. Ozette discoveries would be "a gift from the past," as Makah elder Helen Peterson expressed it. Artifacts would remain with the tribe, not be taken to the university. The tribe would provide space for study, storage, and a preservation lab in Neah Bay. The council voted to join Daugherty in appealing directly to Senator Henry M. Jackson, and through his efforts seventy thousand dollars from the Bureau of Indian Affairs was transferred to the National Park Service and made available to carry the Ozette project through the summer.

The next problem was the preparation for an excavation expected to last all summer and into autumn (and which actually lasted for eleven years). Daugherty could not stay at the coast indefinitely, but he recruited Gerald Grosso as operations manager to set up a camp. A newspaper journalist from the Puget Sound town of Port Orchard, Grosso had worked with the Ozette team from the first, helping with the 1966 trench and again with the 1967 excavation. He knew archaeology, and he knew how to build cabins, plan a water system, and arrange for food and supplies at a site far from the nearest road. Tons of equipment were needed, and again the Coast Guard made airlifts. Later the Marine Air Reserve took over. The flights gave the reservists experience in loading, transporting, and unloading all manner of materials—lumber, roofing paper, stoves, propane tanks, pumps, barrels of gasoline, hoses, and

While his family drums and sings, Jeff Hottowe dances at Neah Bay in the replicated Ozette house.

Northwest Coast Culture

The beat of drums, the words of songs, the movement of dancers, the display of family regalia . . . All of these *did* and *do* characterize Northwest Coast native culture. Geographically, the culture belongs to the roughly fifteen hundred miles of coast that stretches from southeast Alaska to Northern California, much of it still roadless. Cool summers and mild, wet winters define the climate. Many beaches are sandy, many are rocky. Back from the coast, forest-lands stretch like a shaggy green carpet. Berries flourish, readily available to be picked, and edible bulbs and roots await digging. Scores of fish species swim the rivers and the ocean, salmon and halibut the chief among them. Fur seals and whales migrate offshore. Sea otters—overhunted as a trade item between natives and Euro-American newcomers—are making a comeback. Geese and ducks and swans, puffins and murres, gulls and cormorants and eagles and ravens abound.

People have lived along this coast for more than ten thousand years, accord-ing to archaeological evidence. They had no agriculture, the usual economic base for aboriginal village life; they were hunter-fisher-gatherers, yet they lived in plank houses that were large and sturdy, and traveled in dugout canoes forty feet long—or even longer—each capable of carrying twenty to thirty people. Social standing depended on claims to ancestry reaching back to when mythic beings took off their masks and became human. Chiefs headed kinship groups but were not monarchs. They directed use of resource areas they owned, and they held prestigious hereditary rights to rituals and ceremonial regalia. Commoners lived in the houses of chiefly kin and were free to move from one to another according to the work to be done. Slaves performed menial tasks and had no rights, no legacy. They generally were treated well but remained lifelong property, belonging wholly to their owners unless ransomed by their families.

For millennia the culture evolved, retaining its orientation to the sea and expressing, through art, the link of the human world with the spirit world. Then came a veritable wringer of cultural change. Forty-five distinct languages plus variants and dialects were spoken along the coast, but newcomers insisted on English. Missionaries and governments preempted resources and restructured the social order for administrative convenience. Formerly unknown diseases wrought havoc with the hereditary system: they left no one alive with the right to certain respected names and prerogatives. At the same time, the subsistence base shifted: no longer in direct relationship with the sea and the land, the people came to rely on wages derived from various sorts of labor. Through it all, however, they kept their sanity and the culture adjusted.

Now, art is again expressing the relations between humans and the invisible forces; special programs are reviving the old languages; and formally organized canoe journeys are carrying villagers to annual gatherings hosted by tribes and bands from Oregon to Alaska. The journeys' beginnings date to 1989, when Washington celebrated its centennial as a state. Emmet Oliver, from Quinault, and Frank Brown, from Bella Bella, felt it would not be right to acknowledge the newcomers but leave out the people who had already been living here. Members of seventeen tribal groups paddled to Seattle that year, resting overnight along the way at villages and reservations. From that occasion came the idea of an annual celebration of native culture along the entire Northwest Coast. More than eighty tribes and bands now participate. Plans are made and itineraries coordinated via computer and the Internet. Strict rules require that participants use no drugs or alcohol on the trip; wear lifejackets at all times while on the water; practice bailing out, righting, and climbing back into a capsized canoe; and be accompanied by motorized support boats as a safety precaution. Depending on location, hundreds and even thousands of celebration participants arrive by car as well as by canoe. For nearly a week, events center on traditional feasting, storytelling, *slahal* (Indian gambling), displays of ceremonial regalia and dances, and showy gift presentations. But there may also be softball and modern dancing. The cultural present is interwoven with the past.

The two are one, and together they will shape the future.

so on. The men could practice dealing with the logistics of supplying remote areas, including the suspension of heavy cargo beneath the belly of a helicopter.

For the camp, Grosso picked a place near the 1966 trench and the 1967 excavation of historic houses, and he began building something more substantial than the previous sodden tent camp. Combining driftwood from the beach with plywood and plastic sheeting brought by helicopter, a small crew put up a two-story building to serve as cookhouse, dining room, and sleeping quarters, and as a field laboratory where artifacts and faunal material could be washed, labeled, cata-

Initially, the Coast Guard flew in equipment and supplies and flew out artifacts.

loged, and treated with preservative. Eventually they added several eclectic cabins built partly of cedar shakes hand-split from beach-drift logs and from lumber from deck loads lost off passing cargo ships. At first, light at night was limited to the glow from gasoline pressure lamps; later a generator supplied electricity, which was used sparingly to conserve fuel. Wooden tanks at two seeps on the hillside behind the camp supplied freshwater. A sizeable garden supplied vegetables. No telephone service reached Ozette (cell phones did not yet exist), but radio contact linked the camp to Neah Bay and to a Coast Guard lightship anchored offshore at Umatilla Reef. Messages could be relayed. Word of a particularly interesting—or puzzling—discovery might go from the archaeology camp to the lightship to the laboratory at Neah Bay and from there by phone to Makah officials and Daugherty's office at Washington State University.

PUMPS AND HOSES

Excavation goals were to salvage whatever remained of the cultural material slumping onto the beach, to expose a vertical face along the sea bank and record its stratigraphy, and to assess the likelihood of additional cultural deposits. The planks the men had examined in February stood on edge, and they lapped one another indicating they were remnants of a wall. Furthermore, a little north of the slump and still standing upright in a hole was the base of a rafter support post. It was shimmed with rocks, several of which—to judge by wear patterns—had originally been used as whetstones. A house must have stood there, but it was not the one the 1967 test pit had revealed. The planks and the post remnant made Daugherty wonder if they represented "part of a house, all of a house, the front side, the back side, or what."

Examination of the sea bank revealed a complex layering of cultural deposits

The new camp stood alongside the area to be excavated, which is shown here covered with plastic sheets to prevent deposits from drying.

Cabin walls and roofs were made of cedar shakes hand-split from drift logs.

Tanks of preservative solution held house remains until they could be flown to Neah Bay.

separated by mudflows—a slice of time stretching backward from top to bottom. Artifacts like those excavated in 1967 lay in the uppermost layer. Below it, a mudflow capped deposits from the period of early contact with Euro-American mariners, and in that layer the archaeologists found one blue glass bead, a small piece of copper, and a button. Perhaps it was through direct trade with the strange newcomers that Ozette villagers obtained these items, or perhaps through trade with other native groups who had direct contact. Under that layer was another mudflow, and under it were the remains of the demolished house now eroding onto the beach. Excavating this lowest level obviously was urgent if more loss was to be avoided; but the overburden was two to three meters thick, and removing it would not be easy or quick. Machines could not be used, nor could shovels. Hand trowels, too, were inappropriate: this mud was clay and it tended to ball up when troweled, making it likely that small objects would be scraped aside and lost. Also, a metal edge might cut into a buried basket or damage a wooden carving, without even the most careful excavator knowing it was there.

Water proved the answer. Pump it up from the ocean and use fire hoses with as much as 250 pounds of pressure to wash away the heavy mud blanketing the house. Then gently spray the area with garden hoses to safely free even delicate artifacts. Excavating with water was not a new way of removing large amounts of dirt. It had been used by placer miners throughout the West, and for urban regrading projects in, for example, Seattle and Port Angeles. Daugherty and Rice had tested its effectiveness for archaeology at the Hoko River, east of Neah Bay, where baskets were washing out of the bank. The principle of excavating with water was familiar, but putting it into practice at Ozette caused many headaches. Time and again waves rolling in over the reef tore out the hoses that served the pumps, and a crewman would have to pull on a wet suit and struggle out through the surging water to salvage what he could, then reset it all when calm had been restored. Sometimes seaweed clogged the pumps, and once stinging jellyfish spattered out of the hoses, burning Grosso's arms and, from then on, requiring excavators to wear goggles.

The mudflow—glacial outwash—was cohesive and difficult to work through. Its clay particles, smaller than sand or silt particles, had formed a solid deposit, but one with a high water content and held together only by the surface tension of the water molecules. In such cases, when something like an earthquake, or even footsteps, disturbs that delicate balance, what was solid becomes a liquid and flows, or on flat land it becomes "quick sand." Judging by the gradient at Ozette, a soils expert estimated a velocity of sixty miles per hour for the deposit blanketing the old house—and it had been a mudflow, not a mudslide; the clay had *flowed* as a liquid, not *slid* as a solid. The best way to cut through it, the camp log recorded, was "to angle the water stream from the hose at about 20 degrees to the surface and let it bore a hole, then work in

Water from high-pressure hoses washed away the mud overburden blanketing the old house.

Gentle spray freed artifacts without damaging them.

the hose with a slight oscillating motion. The clay breaks off in chunks. It is sterile" (that is, holds nothing of cultural origin).

With the mudflow deposit as much as three meters deep in places, the crew began hydraulic excavation on a scale never before attempted by archaeologists. To protect the reef, runoff water carrying mudflow sediment was directed into large holding ponds at the base of the slope, and there it filtered through beach sand, dropping sediment from the excavation and leaving it to be washed away by winter storms. Students worked rain or shine, without much caring what sort of weather a day brought. The hoses splashed so much that at times everybody wore waterproof clothing anyway. Even school groups and families who had read of the dig and hiked out to see for themselves got spattered. Lance Wilke—a Makah high school student at the time, later highly regarded as a carver—commented that when he first went to Ozette he thought, "Oh boy, what a mess! The mud was up to your knees."

Near the bottom of the mudflow, broken boards, a few artifacts, and chunks of displaced midden began appearing, and at that point excavation switched from high-pressure hoses to garden hoses. The system worked well, although frequently at low tide the pumps could not supply enough water for even the gentlest spray, hence a sober note in the July daily log: "Low tide was at the unreasonable hour of 9:00 A.M. and there was no water to run the pumps. . . . So we are countering by changing work hours to 1:00 P.M. until dark."

HOUSE 1

Here was a house buried centuries ago—the posts and planks it was built of, the benches lining the walls, the cooking hearths, storage boxes, baskets, mats, harpoons,

A replica of the house buried at Ozette was built in Neah Bay.

Withes tied the overlapping wallboards in place.

fishhooks, bows, arrows, tool kits, animal bones—all buried in a jumble that needed to be systematically untangled. The procedure called for excavating according to a surveyed grid of two-meter squares. The system lets archaeologists record the precise location of each piece they lift from the earth and also record where each stratigraphic drawing of an excavation wall originated. Usually archaeologists must piece together the past from scattered indications such as weapons that got lost or were left behind as hunters shifted camp, or from refuse, or from household goods abandoned when people moved on. Usually stone and bone and shell are all that remain, as had been true in the trench at Ozette. But this house, apparently prehistoric, still had its structural elements and its household furnishings and possessions. They ranged from ceremonial artwork to objects as mundane as sticks to use as tongs when lifting hot stones from a fire into a cooking box filled with water. There were even leaves still green when first uncovered, although they turned brown within seconds of exposure to air.

Seemingly the house had been lived in for generations, perhaps a century or more. Its floor deposits were thick, and what remained of the walls (and the walls of other houses found later) showed termite or carpenter ant damage. A break in one wall had been remedied by covering it with a whale's scapula. A canoe paddle strengthened part of another wall. In a third, a roof board was substituting for a wallboard; the parallel grooves running the length of its surface were originally intended to channel rain runoff. A bench made of a plank nearly a meter wide had split and been laced back together by drilling holes and running a cord through them.

The six-centimeter-long head of a wooden carving protruded from an excavation wall and was overlooked throughout the winter; exposed to air, it cracked. The body, still buried, remained preserved.

As summer segued into fall, it was obvious that the project could not be quickly finished, and that the site could not be left unattended through the winter lest artifacts again be lost by erosion or carried off by hikers. The quantity, quality, and variety of artifacts and the cultural understanding generated by the excavation so impressed an archaeologist from the Smithsonian that he told a newspaper reporter he considered Ozette "the most significant and unique find in Northwest Coast archaeology, truly a national treasure," and a Canadian archaeologist from the National Museum of Man spoke of it as "the most important archaeological site on the coast." Clearly, the phone call from the Makah Tribal Council had initiated a project that needed years to complete.

For the fall and winter, a crew of only five or six stayed at Ozette. Funds were running out, and although the university supplied equipment and groceries, there was no money for salaries. A visiting fifth-grade class from Forks "took up a collection and gave us $7.09," the camp log noted, and a Seattle art society sent a donation. Ozette offered a chance to find carvings and other wooden objects from a time before Euro-Americans arrived, exploring and collecting; nobody interested in art could let such a chance to see the past slip away for a lack of dollars. Other donors gave their time, cooking or typing up reports so that the archaeologists could devote full energy to the excavation, and a doctor and his wife came every weekend from Seattle to attend to medical needs. The Makah Tribe sent groceries and arranged for students to take time out from class and help at Ozette for a few weeks at a stretch. Two gifts of five thousand dollars each came from wealthy businessmen. The Marine Air Reserve continued helicopter service, and Julia Butler Hansen (the congressional representative from southwest Washington and head of the House Appropriations Committee for Interior Affairs) worked tirelessly to arrange proper funding through the National Park Service so that the research could go forward. When she finally succeeded, word was relayed to the archaeology site by radio through the Coast Guard lightship, and the entry in the camp log reads, "Real celebration tonight."

The September 16, 1970, log entry reads, "Continued excavation in the house. Found several flattened wooden boxes in Square 70, Unit V, one with remains of what seems to be a blanket, white with blue-black plaid design. Radio message sent to Daugherty on what to do with it. MSG came back not to clean or unfold, keep moist, wrap in plastic, and get to Pullman ASAP." The blanket was fragile but what inspection was possible seemed to show the fiber used to weave it probably included the seed fluff of cattail or fireweed to augment dog hair, in common use by some Northwest Coast weavers but not previously known among Makahs. Eventually the mix was identified as feathers, cedar bark, and moss spun with animal hair, almost surely dog. The standard procedure with all artifacts was to hold them at the field laboratory until the marines could fly them to the Neah Bay lab, but this one was to go to Washington State University's Laboratory of Anthropology, where Daugherty hoped x-rays might reveal whether anything was folded inside. Consequently, wrapped in plastic, the blanket went into a backpack and three students headed down the beach to the trail and began the long trip to Pullman. After being x-rayed, the blanket would be treated with a mold preventative and put into a freezer for safekeeping. Unfolding it was tempting, but that might destroy it. No other prehistoric plaid pattern was known along the Northwest Coast. "It's like having a Christmas present you can't open," Professor Daugherty sighed—and to his disappointment, the x-rays showed nothing in the bundle.

So far, the number of baskets in the old house totaled fifty. They included baskets for dried fish, clam baskets with an open weave to allow water to drain, and small woven pouches still holding fishhooks, along with bone points to be bound onto wooden shanks for more fishhooks. There also were whetstones for sharpening the points. Another basket seemed to be a kit. Somebody had finished work and set it down; then centuries later Daugherty's and Grosso's hands were the next to touch it. Using the gentlest possible spray, they began freeing the contents. First to come out was a wooden whorl from a weaver's spindle, next two combs, then awls that were scattered throughout the basket, and a bundle of bird bones along with a whetstone. Probably the bones were meant to be made into more awls. Other items included stone blades, a lump of red pigment, and clumps of indistinguishable fiber, perhaps intended for spinning into thread. Apparently this was a weaver's kit.

Another discovery took several days to uncover. The entry in the log for October 3 reads, "Found a piece of carved wood set with teeth. Appears to be part of a feast bowl. Box removed from under it, also a canoe paddle." Parts of the object lay scattered in three adjacent excavation squares, and the crew took four days to free them. The log then recorded, "Big wooden object assembled. Pix taken and press release made. It's not a bowl, but a carving in the shape of a whale's fin. Size, about 80 centimeters wide and 80 high with Thunderbird and other designs set in teeth and painted red and black." The teeth were sea otter—seven hundred of them. Most were molars, although canines were set along the edge to give a jagged, saw-blade effect. Prestige and some sort of ceremony must have been associated with such an elaborate object, but what ceremony? Written records make no mention of anything similar, and none of the Makahs could remember their elders speaking of such a carving. The only available clue came from a historical source. An etching made by the official artist for Captain James Cook's voyage of discovery in the late 1700s shows a carved whale fin in a house at Nootka, on Vancouver Island. At Ozette, a small piece of a second whale-fin effigy was also found, this one decorated not with sea otter teeth but with snail opercula, the snug-fitting "doors" that snails clamp shut to hold in their moisture at low tide.

A cedar carving of a whale fin inlaid with sea otter teeth must have been used ceremonially. A Smithsonian Institution recording of historic Makah songs includes "Song of a Gathering at which a Whale Fin Is Displayed."

In the Neah Bay laboratory, Gerald Grosso (right) and Makah student Hamon Ides reassembled the whale-fin carving smashed by the mudflow.

Discoveries came daily now, and camp operations were comfortably established, albeit with occasional reminders of Ozette's wilderness location. Under the heading "Happenings," the camp log one day recorded, "Jim caught Mr. Civet Cat [a skunk]," and another day it commented, "Frogs and crickets made a lot of noise." Cougar tracks printed the sandspit at Ch'kknow acht Island, and a marauding bear persisted in breaking into cabins, including "the men's dorm while occupied. Fred [the camp dog] had a barking fit . . . but the bear didn't seem to care and walked right in on us. After that we all slept in the mess hall till the bear could be tranquilized [and relocated]." The marines continued to bring food and other supplies except when storms or fog forestalled them. Students also packed food down the trail and tended the vegetable garden. The beach itself provided part of the crew's needs. They dug clams at low tide, trapped crabs on the reef, and caught strange, goggle-eyed bottom fish with hook and line. Firewood for combating the damp cold came from drift logs jackstrawed by surf on the upper beach—and cutting and hauling the wood to camp deepened everyone's awareness of what life had been like for Ozette villagers. Even with a chain saw, garnering wood took time and hard work. Daugherty won-

Gerald Grosso (left), John Mobley, and Richard Daugherty gingerly opened a weaver's kit holding a comb, a spindle whorl, and awls.

A large comb lay among the items in the basket.

dered whether the abundance of logs washed from the forest by rivers and brought to the beach by ocean currents affected coast dwellers' choice of certain locations as camping places or village sites. The amount of work involved in getting fuel perhaps helped explain something else as well. Early photographs of Ozette show that the forest had been cleared from the slope behind the village. This must have increased its instability and contributed to the causes of the mudflows.

By the spring of 1971, visitors occasionally numbered more than one hundred a day. School classes from throughout Washington hiked out to see the buried house. A physicist and his wife came from faraway Switzerland after reading about Ozette in their newspaper. Archaeologists from several universities and agencies repeatedly hiked in to watch the excavation's progress. Indian people came from La Push, from the Yakama reservation in central Washington, and from several villages in British Columbia. One day ten seniors from the Makah Club visited, accompanied "by about 80 grade school youngsters," according to the camp log. Another time Makah Hugh Smith, age sixty, arrived from Neah Bay in a fourteen-foot open boat and "spent the day . . . looking at artifacts, drinking coffee, eating lunch, telling stories, giving ideas on use of some artifacts, expressing general approval and amazement at [our] work." Also from Neah Bay was Roger Colfax, who hiked in. "He lived here in 1912–1914," notes the log. "He reminisced on fishing, food eaten. Said he is amazed to realize he lived on top of all 'these old things.' Gave Makah names for islands: Ozette—*Wa'eaq*; Bodeltha—*Badiltha*; Cannonball—*Ch'kknow acht.*"

By summer, excavation of the house had been under way for just over a year. More than twenty thousand people had slogged through the mud of the forest and dodged the waves lapping the beach to reach the site, and almost five thousand artifacts had been recovered. Particularly notable was part of a plank about a half meter wide and three meters long, lying face up. On it were the carved outlines of the head, back, and tail of a wolf or some other doglike animal, and the eye and beak of a bird, probably a thunderbird. Days later what was assumed to be the rest of the plank was found and the carvings seemed complete. But still later a fragmented, mirror-image carving of another wolf and thunderbird was discovered. In the old house the complete plank probably had served as a prestigious wall panel or a partition board separating one family's living area from that of another family.

A year later—June 1972—a second carved plank was found, this one in the northeast corner of the house, opposite of where the wolves-and-thunderbirds plank had lain. The first hint of it came when students in the lab were cleaning lengths of wood apparently split from a plank. They noticed faint incised lines and wondered whether these pieces might be part of another carved plank. They checked the numbered tags keying each fragment to where it had come from in the excavation, and then spread

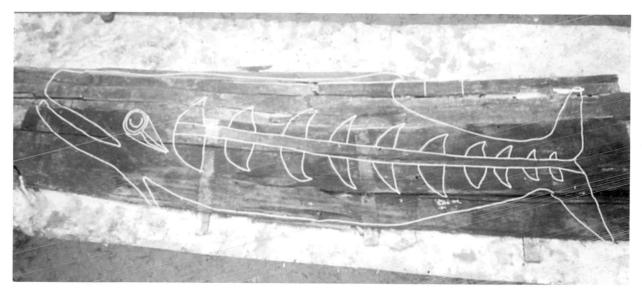

Recovered and reassembled, a wall panel measuring five meters long displays pairs of thunderbirds and wolves, spirit beings of great power.

A carving of a whale a little more than five meters long took several days to excavate. Here, its shallow lines are emphasized with string.

the word to watch for additional pieces. There might be more of them near where the pieces already sent to the lab had lain, or perhaps at a distance from them, swept along by the force of the mudflow. Actually, part of a wide plank was already partly exposed but had not been excavated further because of artifacts lying on top of it still encased in mud. Daugherty decided to gently wash beneath the plank, clearing enough of the mud to feel the undersurface. Reaching in, he touched grooves cut into the wood. Curiosity rose. There definitely was carving, but what would it be? Daugherty's journal entry for June 16 is a model of restraint: "Dug clams. . . . Worked in NE corner [of the house]. Discovered a carved plank."

Days of work lay ahead before the plank could be turned over to reveal its carving. A pair of poles, for some reason lashed together, protruded from the mud above the plank. So did a canoe paddle, a whale scapula, and a broken roof board. These were freed, photographed, drawn, lifted, and sent to the field lab. Under them was a box and a bundle of boughs of about finger thickness, probably material to twine into a burden basket or perhaps a fish trap. Then came two wooden wedges of the type used to split boards from cedar logs, and a stone maul. Next was a wooden food dish about the size and shape of a modern serving platter; a spear for catching salmon; and part of a rake used for herring, small fish that swarm into shallow water in great numbers and are easily caught. It took a week to clear the plank, which was huge—five meters long by one meter wide. Finally, it could be lifted. Students sandwiched the plank between pairs of sturdy slats, one slipped underneath and one laid on top. They lifted, carried the plank to the field lab, and turned it over. The carving was a whale. It too must have belonged to a high-ranking family, possibly one headed by a whaler.

September came. For more than two years, clearing the shroud of mud from the old house had proceeded methodically, but the location of the north wall was still unknown. Daugherty had arranged a year's leave from his on-campus responsibilities at Washington State University so as to engage in hands-on work at Ozette. The leave also gave respite from, in his words, constantly "either going to or coming from the site, hiking in or hiking out." Now the leave was up. Gerald Grosso had moved to the lab in Neah Bay to handle the preservation and storage of artifacts. Paul Gleeson, a graduate student, took over as field director.

Makah Days, 1972

To help celebrate Makah Days, the yearly recognition of when the tribe was officially presented with a United States flag, the marines sometimes

Richard Daugherty escorted Makah senior citizens arriving at Ozette by helicopter.

made a special flight carrying senior citizens from Neah Bay to Ozette. The year 1972 brought extra reason to celebrate. Tribal ownership of the land at Ozette had finally been clearly established.

Nora Barker

What happened was this: In 1855 the government knew so little about the people whose lives and lands it was rearranging that treaty negotiators failed to recognize Ozette as the southernmost of the Makahs' five main villages. Consequently, no land was set aside there by treaty, although in the 1890s an executive order deeded seven hundred acres to the Makahs as a detached reservation. In the early 1930s, however, families had moved from there to Neah Bay because the government threatened to jail parents who did not send their children to school, yet provided none at Ozette. The houses stood empty except for use as a seasonal fishing or seal-hunting camp, and in the 1960s the government announced its intention to abolish the Ozette Reservation unless the Makahs "could prove entitlement."

Part of that proof came from elders who testified to having lived at Ozette as children, and the archaeological excavations substantiated those memories. "Maybe that's my great-great grandma's stuff" is how Isabell Ides put it, and Luke Markishtum pointed out, "The artifacts are recognized by elders and others of our people as things that they have used and known. . . . And that is the picture that we set before the United States Congress in getting that land [clearly conveyed into] the Makahs' ownership."

Finally the struggle had ended. Ozette was again properly recognized as Makah, and for a few hours senior citizens watched waves wash ashore there and heard the cries of gulls and eagles. The trail to the beach was too rough and long for their aging legs, and they had thought they would never again see their old village site. But here they were!

Helen Peterson spoke for them all when she said, "It's been over fifty years since I was at Ozette, and I've really missed this beach." The flight to the site had lasted little more than fifteen minutes, but that had been long enough for the seniors to make up a song about a huge bird with whirling wings and a blinking red eye, carrying humans in its belly. "We left in canoes," Nora Barker said, "and today we have come back in a helicopter."

Some excavation squares, measuring two meters by two meters, held as many as four hundred artifacts and pieces of artifacts in house-floor deposits less than fifty centimeters deep. (Note whale bones at lower right.)

Chapter Three

More Discoveries

THE LABORATORY IN NEAH BAY

MAKAH ELDER LLOYD COLFAX ONCE COMMENTED, "BEING INDIAN FORCES a person to not have a history except as part of the people who have conquered you. You become part of their history." The archaeology work at Ozette was partly countering the truth of this statement by providing physical evidence of the Makahs' past, and tribal members were participating in the process. Makah students joined archaeology crews, and senior citizens reminisced about objects like those coming from Ozette, familiar to them from their younger days. They also recognized objects their grandparents had described or had kept stored in the attic, treasured but no longer used. Such input from direct descendants of the people being studied archaeologically is exceedingly rare. The elders could explain artifacts such as beaver-tooth dice that belonged to a gambling game played by women, and the wooden paddles that look much like today's ping-pong paddles but were for hitting shuttlecocks of salmonberry stems and feathers into the air as the player counted the number of successes before missing.

By the end of summer 1972 a remarkable thirteen thousand artifacts and pieces of artifacts had been flown from the excavation site to a laboratory and storage facility provided by the tribe in Neah Bay, and there the seniors often gathered to see the latest discoveries. Daugherty called the facility "the finest lab an archaeologist has ever had so close to his excavation." It had sinks and work benches, tanks to hold artifacts soaking in preservative solutions, thousands of feet of storage shelves, an apartment for lab manager Gerald Grosso and his wife—everything needed to care for artifacts ranging from huge and heavy cedar house planks to wooden bowls and delicate combs and baskets. The lab was where objects from the excavation were sta-

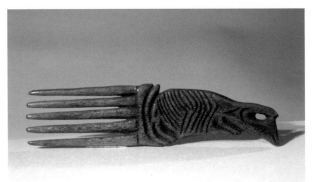

bilized and preserved, and part of the challenge was to adapt established laboratory methods and advice from other laboratories to Ozette realities. As they came from the excavation, artifacts and structural remains from the old house were carried to the field lab for preliminary treatment. Then they went into a preservative solution of 50 percent water and 50 percent Carbowax (the commercial name for one type of polyethylene glycol) to await transport to Neah Bay, where they continued to soak, some of them for months or even years. Staying constantly saturated in the wet mud at Ozette had leached out some of the wood's constituents. That left little but water to support remaining cellular material; and if it were to evaporate, the cells would collapse and the wood would shrink or crack. Carbowax counters the problem by replacing the water with a stable scaffold for the remaining cellular components.

By 1976 the number of artifacts from Ozette had grown to almost forty thousand, and awareness of Ozette had spread so widely that an international Wet Wood Conservation Conference convened in Neah Bay despite the village's remote location 152 miles west of Seattle by ferry and a narrow, twisting road. As an announcement of the conference said, the goal was "to make available the best information in the world on the state of the art of conservation of wood." Attendees came not just from the

Beaver-tooth dice (*top left*). Makah elders remembered a women's game played with such dice.

Makah elders thought women used bone combs for pinning up braided hair, wooden ones for grooming hair. Other combs were used for scratching and for combing dogs' hair. Combs shown here measure eleven to fourteen centimeters long.

United States and neighboring Canada but also from Sweden, Denmark, England, Australia, and the African nation Ivory Coast. Funding was supplied by the Smithsonian Institution, the National Endowment for the Arts, the Makah Tribe, and Washington State University.

At the time, few wet sites anywhere in the world had been excavated. Archaeologists knew about the human bodies found in bogs in northern Europe and Great Britain, and the remnants of lakeside habitations in Switzerland. There also were unexpectedly intact sunken ships found in Scandinavia dating as far back as the Viking period, A.D. 300 to 1100; and in North America, waterlogged sites along the gulf coast of Florida held a range of objects, from carved and painted wooden masks to dugout canoes. Now excavation of the centuries-old whaling village at Ozette was being added to the list of world wet sites. Its yield of wood, bark, root, and twig provided a major opportunity to contribute to the science of preserving waterlogged wooden artifacts, and in large measure doing so meant pioneering laboratory methods, much as hydraulic excavation methods had been pioneered at the site.

More than 90 percent of the artifacts were made of softwoods, such as red cedar, spruce, and yew. Soaking in Carbowax worked well for them, but there also were artifacts made of hardwoods such as alder, maple, and crab apple, and they defied Grosso's preservation efforts. He tried gently heating a representative sample of these for an hour a day in an increasingly concentrated solution of Carbowax, but that had no apparent benefit. He also tried periodically diluting the solution by adding hot water, then letting it evaporate and thereby slowly raise the concentration of Carbowax. Such tests stretched over periods of a year or more with some successes and some disappointments. Evidently the kind of wood—hardwood or softwood—was only part of the answer. This led Grosso to wonder whether how the "problem artifacts"

A wooden bowl twenty-nine centimeters long still has its braid of human hair, a rare example of animal tissue other than bones and teeth having been preserved.

had been used might hold the key. Canoe paddles and tool handles might still be oily from the hands that had gripped them. Small wooden bowls might also be oily; they must once have held seal oil and whale oil, remembered by Makah elders as a dipping sauce for dried fish. Grosso reasoned that the oil might have saturated the surface of these bowls so much that nothing could force wax into the wood. Soaking them for months, heating them in Carbowax, experimenting with different strengths of the solution and different molecular weights of the Carbowax—nothing worked. The wood still cracked when taken from the tanks for even a few minutes.

Grosso kept trying. He tested techniques being developed abroad and discussed at the Neah Bay conference. One attempt incorporated the acetone-and-gum-rosin process originated at the National Museum of Antiquities in Scotland. Unfortunately, although the tested bowl looked restored, it had turned brittle. That might be disastrous if it were to fall. Grosso sent another problem hardwood bowl to the National University of Australia. It had soaked for six years in the Neah Bay lab but persisted in cracking when taken out of preservative. In Australia it was first frozen, then vacuum-dried. Result? It too had become brittle and, furthermore, had turned an unnatural light tan color. That outcome was all too familiar: Grosso needed to try something else.

FINISHING HOUSE 1

Funding remained ever precarious, and Daugherty was spending a week at a time in Washington, D.C., attending to political realities. The Ozette project that at first was expected to take a few months had become instead an ongoing, year-round undertaking. Without funds it could not continue. Daugherty served on the four-man National Committee for the Recovery of Archaeological Remains and had been appointed by President Lyndon Johnson to the newly created Advisory Council on Historic Preservation. He also continued working with congressional representatives in Washington, D.C.: Julia Butler Hansen, chair of the House Appropriations Committee for Interior Affairs, and Lloyd Meads, chairman of the Subcommittee on Indian Affairs; as well as with Senators Warren Magnuson, head of the Senate Appropriations Committee, and Henry Jackson, head of the Committee on Interior Affairs. Joined by Makah tribal members, he urged that the budget of the archaeology program administered by the National Park Service include money specifically for Ozette.

The unique character of the site had become widely recognized. Summers brought field-school crews of thirty to forty undergraduate college students, augmented by archaeology graduate students, Makahs, and volunteers from throughout the country who donated time and talent. In fall, winter, and spring, small crews of six to

Without continuing service by U.S. Marines helicopter, the archaeology camp would have been too remote for getting supplies in and artifacts out.

ten safeguarded the site, continuing to painstakingly free the buried house and to patiently sort the thousands of animal bones and shells taken from the excavation. Recruitment was never a problem, despite a letter sent to all applicants telling them that the excavation site was four miles from the nearest road and had no telephone, and that they should bring "good rain gear and rain boots, backpack, hiking boots, and warm clothes. . . . We work through rain, howling gales, and whatever."

Year-round, the marines flew in supplies and flew artifacts out to the Neah Bay lab. "So there we were engaged in our various chores when the sky opens up and drops a helicopter on us," reads a camp log entry. "It's got Marines and Carbowax but no eggs, no onions, no Wesson oil, no meat, no fruits. I love the Marines. They're coming again tomorrow." And the next day the log reported: "Chopper came with 3 million tons of food & stuff. And there tucked away in the landing gear was contraband ice cream!"

Daugherty and field director Paul Gleeson had expected to finish excavating House 1 by the fall of 1973, but it was 1975 before that goal was reached. The extended time actually derived less from problems than from the surfeit of physical remains of the house structure along with the implements of daily lives. Many artifacts were in use when the mudflow struck, or were still in the process of being manufactured. Several showed repairs. Others had been discarded or lost. Whole classes of artifacts had never before been seen in an archaeological context, nor were they represented in museum collections or ethnographic accounts. Researchers at Ozette could examine not just objects and chronology but also patterns of behavior: which of their avail-

One of the students uncovered wooden clubs and canoe paddles lying beside part of a loom. The paddles are sharply pointed to control dripping while in use; drips might be noisy enough to disturb basking prey.

A wooden carving lay with braided cordage and the handle of a paddle.

able resources did the villagers prefer, and how did they obtain, process, store, and use them? The buried house offered a direct look into the past, free of the possible bias of early ethnographic reports.

When the north wall finally was reached, House 1 dimensions proved to be an impressive twenty meters long and ten meters wide. Probably it had sheltered twenty to forty people, all of them related, and each nuclear family would have had its own designated space. The house had no windows and only one door, but by using a long pole to lift a roof plank and set it aside, smoke could be allowed to escape and daylight to brighten the house interior. Benches for sleeping and for use as work space ringed the interior. They were set a half meter or so from the wall and supported by stakes driven into the floor. A set of these stakes along the south wall was angled and broken, showing the direction of the mudflow and its catastrophic force.

Space behind the benches provided room for storage, and this is where archaeologists found the greatest concentration of artifacts. Partly this was a result of the deliberate use of the space for storage and partly a result of less housecleaning done behind the benches than in the rest of the house. This lack of housecleaning allowed, in Gleeson's words, "meaningful scraps from the manufacturing process" to accumulate where artisans had sat working with their tools. Excavating the jumble of artifacts, raw materials, and debris was often akin to working on a three-dimensional puzzle with the pieces scattered through a layer of heavy, wet clay. Progress came slowly. Each two-by-two-meter excavation square took about fifty person-days of careful spraying and stopping to record, photograph, and survey the location of each item as it lay in place. Behind one bench, for example, were a storage box barely visible amid a mishmash of wallboards, and two arrows broken against its corner. Seemingly the arrows had been snapped by the rush of the mudflow. The boards and arrows had to be dealt with before touching the box. When it finally was worked free and opened, it was found to hold materials for making fishhooks—bits of bone, a whetstone, fine cord wound around sticks, and some finished hooks.

Beneath another bench, archaeologists found a basket, a canoe paddle, two seal clubs, a bow, a length of braided cordage, and a loom. The archaeologists were especially interested in the loom, the first of seven found at Ozette. With the looms were a total of twenty-three spindle whorls and ten weaver's battens (long, thin, sword-shaped sticks used to beat fibers before they were spun). Cedar-bark strings still lying parallel gave additional evidence of weaving. All that remained of a blanket, the strings were the warp that once held a weft probably made of dog hair. Mundane to the eye, they actually constituted a link to an often overlooked cultural attribute. People along the central part of the Northwest Coast are rightly known as proficient hunters, fishers, and gatherers. They also practiced animal husbandry: they bred small Samoyed-like dogs specifically for their hair, typically keeping them on offshore islands to prevent their mixing with the larger village dogs used in hunting. The Ozette discovery of weaving implements confirmed historic and ethnographic reports of wool dogs and established that the practice was older than previously known. British Captain George Vancouver in 1778 described their fleece as "a mixture of a very coarse kind of wool with fine long hair capable of being spun into yarn," and he mentioned once seeing forty of the dogs being herded along the beach. The dogs, probably now extinct, and the alpacas kept by Peruvian Incas, are the only native animal species in the prehistoric Americas known to have been domesticated as a source of fiber for textiles. Mountain goat wool, widely used by Northwest Coast weavers, would have been available at Ozette only

Makah student Melissa Peterson used a replica loom to weave a sample copy of the plaid blanket found in House 1.

Wooden battens, measuring seventy-four to ninety-three centimeters long, were used to clean shorn wool by beating it before it was spun into yarn. A special breed of dog provided an outer coat of three-inch hair and a woolly undercoat.

through trade. The goats were not native to Washington's Olympic Peninsula; those there now are descended from goats introduced in the early 1900s.

Metal was another discovery of special interest: House 1 held twenty-eight tools with metal blades and an additional fourteen wooden hafts stained by blades that had completely rusted away. Daugherty and Gleeson had not really expected to make such a discovery in a prehistoric house, but neither were they wholly surprised. Written accounts of late-1700s coastal explorations from the Aleutian Islands to Northern California consistently mention small amounts of highly prized iron or steel already in possession of the natives. A description by Friar Miguel de la Campa, who traveled with Spanish explorer Bruno Heceta in 1775, is representative. De la Campa describes an encounter with a California native who "by very expressive signs" indicated he had made a knife "from a nail which he found in a piece of wreckage and had beaten out with a stone." Quite surely Japan was the original source of such metal, and ocean currents the delivery mechanism. An iron age began in Japan as early as the first century A.D., judging not from actual metal blades but from the telltale scars they left on wood. Written records from a millennium later indicate hundreds of small, charcoal-burning smelters processing naturally occurring, iron-rich beach sand in Japan. Bits of wreckage with various iron or steel fittings, along with occasional intact vessels, are known to have drifted across the Pacific and washed ashore in North America in historic time. They must also have done so in prehistoric time. In the official phase-5 project report for October 1972 to July 1973, Grosso reported on a metallurgical laboratory's test of Ozette blades. It found them to be made of "extremely pure" iron with a high carbon content—in other words, steel. Furthermore, the blades' trace elements were similar to those of Japanese samurai swords, several of which the lab had, by chance, recently tested. The large number of metal tools at Ozette led Gleeson to speculate that some may even have been given away at potlatches or used as trade items along with other valuable resources.

Perhaps the most interesting part of the entire house was its interior northeast

Metal tools reached Ozette before Euro-American mariners started to arrive in the late eighteenth century. Quite surely the metal came from Japan. The blade of this tool is seventeen and one-half centimeters long.

The largest metal tool found at Ozette measures a total of almost fifty-three centimeters long. Makah elders thought it might have been used for cutting blubber from whales.

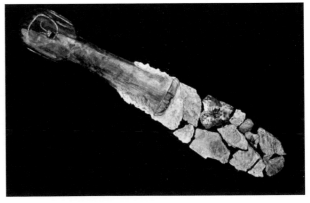

corner. There, a large hearth that was set two to four meters from the wall must have been used on ceremonial occasions. Its placement seemed purposeful. It would prevent flames from licking wall planks or roof support posts and beams even if the host family chose to display wealth by pouring seal or whale oil on the fire. Such flagrant demonstrations are recorded ethnographically; they brag of wealth so vast it could be squandered.

Not far from the House 1 hearth lay something large and flat, woven of cedar bark in a simple checker-weave style. At first the best guess was that this might be part of a canoe sail. But when it was finally washed free, the daily log recorded that the discovery "turned out to be 2 large harpooner's pouches with 3 harpoon blades each." The pouches measured ninety by seventy centimeters and appeared to have been hung together from a rafter. The blades were made of the heavy shell of California mussels, common on the reef offshore from Ozette. Each was fitted with a pair of elk-antler barbs tied in place with cordage that was kept tight by the insertion of tiny wooden wedges. A protective strip of folded cedar bark encased each harpoon point, its ends split and woven to prevent fraying. A whaler's family must have lived in this part of the house, the most prestigious of its inhabitants and possibly of the entire village. The huge wall panel carved with a whale came from this corner. So did the cedar-bark hat with a telltale knobbed crown marking it as the property of a person of high rank. There also were 254 highly valued dentalia shells, probably once strung as a necklace, and a bench with its front edge inlaid with the opercula of 199 red turban snails, a species not found locally and therefore suggesting trade. And there were whale barnacles, seemingly uninteresting but actually evidence of meals rich with blubber and whale meat. The barnacles, about the size and shape of a golf ball cut in half, attach themselves as larvae on the skin of gray and humpback whales and feed by filtering plankton out of the water. Their presence in the house pointed to long-ago—and repeated—success in paddling out from Ozette, harpooning a whale, towing it to the village beach, butchering it, and carrying a portion into House 1.

A large cedar-bark pouch held mussel-shell blades for harpooning whales.

MORE HOUSES

The start of the excavation of House 1 had been dictated by the winter storm waves undercutting the sea bank and exposing planks and artifacts—

Richard Daugherty opened a folded cedar-bark sheath holding a harpoon blade.

Mussel-shell harpoon blades were fitted with elk-antler barbs and attached to a heavy line that connected to sealskin floats. The floats slowed and tired a whale after it had been struck.

Whale barnacles in House 1 must have come from a humpback whale; gray-whale barnacles do not preserve well.

Whaling

Makah elder Ada Markishtum remembered:

> We used to wait for when the tide was in, then all go
> down and pull the whale in with ropes. . . . [Once]
> it was nine in the morning when I got down to the beach . . . and they had the
> blubber already off, and the meat. Just the ribs left, sticking up. They had to cut
> it while it was low tide—blubber and meat, and those teeth [baleen]. They were
> for fish gear. And the sinew. You cut it and dried it for thread; then you pounded
> it and wet it and sewed, or used it to fasten a harpoon on the shaft. . . . Oh, the
> whale! You could use it for everything.

Successful whaling depended as much on ritual preparation as on weaponry and skill.

Whaling carried great prestige. It depended on ritual, skill, courage, and
equipment. Whalers were chiefs, and chiefs made the important decisions
about the economic, political, and social concerns of village life. Whaling was
so fundamental to Makah culture that in 1855 the treaty with the United States
government included a guarantee of the continuing right to hunt whales "at
usual and accustomed grounds and stations." Yet by 1928 the tribe stopped
whaling. Commercial hunting had decimated whale populations; and in Neah
Bay, epidemics in the 1800s along with enforced acceptance of mainstream
acculturation had taken a toll on the people.

Fifteen nations joined in forming the International Whaling Commission in 1946, agreeing to regulate their hunts and acknowledging the right of native people to continue subsistence hunts. In 1970 the United States added gray whales to the federal endangered species list, and in 1986 the International Whaling Commission banned commercial whaling to allow populations to rebuild. By 1994 the policy had allowed gray whales to reach their carrying capacity, and they were officially removed from the endangered list. The Makah Tribal Council then notified the National Marine Fisheries Service that they intended to resume whaling as part of "a concerted effort" to reverse the "damage done during the years of forced assimilation." For millennia, whales had provided a subsistence and ceremonial base. Elders remembered their fathers' and grandfathers' tales of whaling. Some still owned whaling gear. Many still knew family rituals of preparation and celebration. They knew the songs and the names that had been "put away" until appropriate for a new generation. Whaling was both a vivid and treasured memory and a legal right. Even so, the tribe chose to abide by modern international and national regulations. Twice the United States government presented the Makahs' case to the International Whaling Commission, and in 1997 the commission agreed that the Makahs could hunt twenty gray whales over the next five years, no more than four of them in any one year.

Modern legalities thus duly observed, the tribe formed its own Whaling Commission with representatives from whaling families. Their task was to oversee preparations for the first hunt in decades. Traditionally on the Northwest Coast, only Alaskan Inuit and Aleut people, as well as Nuchalnuth speakers on the outer coasts of southern Vancouver Island and the northern Olympic Peninsula, hunted whales, although all used the oil and flesh and bones of drift whales. As trade with Euro-Americans had expanded, chiefs increasingly had switched from whale hunting to becoming harbor masters; wealth was coming in a new way, for example, trading sea otter pelts for blankets, muskets, and metal. Next, wealth came in the form of cash wages, which were as readily available to commoners as to chiefs, a radical change. Nonetheless, memory of whaling remained: eight men in a cedar dugout canoe thirty to forty feet long, six men paddling, one steering, one standing and thrusting a harpoon into a whale.

Candidates for the new whaling crew learned the old ways of reading the weather and the ocean currents. They spent long hours paddling a cedar canoe and swimming in the frigid waters of the ocean. Most important of all, they followed their families' spiritual rituals and purification ceremonies. Plans called for the hunt to take place from a traditional canoe, and for the whale to be struck in the traditional way, by a hand-thrust harpoon. But the canoe would be followed by motorized boats with Makah crews ready to assist if needed. Also, immediately after being harpooned, the whale would be killed by a high-caliber rifle shot, a more humane measure than the old way of repeatedly harpooning the whale and letting it tow the canoe until so weakened that it could be dispatched with a special killing lance. Animal rights groups and a few environmental groups—although not the Sierra Club or Greenpeace—swarmed Neah Bay in protest, and media representatives by the dozen sought interviews and camera angles. Regardless, practice for the hunt continued and on Monday, May 17, 1999, whaling plans turned into actuality. Early that morning, paddlers headed out from their camp west of Neah Bay, and offshore from Ozette a young, thirty-foot gray whale surfaced close to them. Theron Parker stood and thrust his harpoon. In that moment the past joined the present.

In Neah Bay, Makah families walked the beach waiting to welcome the whale, and senior citizens sat out of the steady drizzle in cars parked along the upper edge of the beach. Songs and prayers greeted the whale as men hauled it ashore. When Saturday came, the tribe hosted a celebration with a parade, feasting, speeches, dances, and songs. Tribal members living off the reservation came. So did members of neighboring Olympic Peninsula tribes and of tribes from Puget Sound and British Columbia, the Midwest, the Plains—even from Africa! A Masai chieftain spoke eloquently of the worldwide struggle of native people seeking to protect the continuity of their cultural rights, whether Makahs hunting a whale or Masai hunting a lion.

Relatives formally gave Theron Parker a whaler's name, "Getter of the Fin," a reference to the dorsal fin, which is the most prized part of a whale. The celebration began at noon and lasted all night. The Makahs had kept faith with their ancestors.

an act-now-or-lose-it-forever emergency situation. But Daugherty knew that this house was not the only one buried at Ozette. The test pit dug in 1967 while assessing the extent of the village site had revealed evidence of another, and in 1971 he had located two more. One had stood just north of House 1, the other to the east. The mudflow had carried planks and artifacts from both into the wreckage of House 1.

Major drainage problems evidently plagued the residents of what became designated as House 2, up the slope about two meters east of House 1. To prevent the earthen floor of that house from turning into a soggy mess, its residents had constructed an "intriguing and unexpected feature," as the camp log described it.

They had dug two trenches across the floor and lined and covered them with adzed planks. Seemingly this provided an effective drain for runoff from the slope behind the house. But it was a solution that created a problem for the people of House 1. The trenches carried the House 2 drainage to the back wall of House 1, necessitating a floor trench in that house too. It carried the water across the floor, out beneath the south wall, and into a wide ditch filled with whale skulls, vertebrae, and mandibles—a "neighborhood drainage control system" that channeled the seepage to the sea bank and onto the beach. This evidently was an effective enough solution to warrant reconstructing the ditch at least four times, two of them with an almost identical arrangement of whale bones: a pair of skulls at the lower end, next vertebrae, then mandibles.

Artifacts in House 2 reminded the excavation crew of those in House 1. There were 97 whetstones, 159 wooden box sides, 10 tools with metal bits, 23 bundles of boughs and twigs, a large basket with folded cedar bark and a ground slate blade probably used in stripping bark from the trees, infant cradles, a miniature canoe (a toy?), a miniature whale-bone club carved with a thunderbird, and forty-two canoe paddles, including several in various stages of being carved. New as a discovery was a small copper pendant. Perhaps it had been a potlatch gift or was received in trade with people living to

Trenches carried drainage across the floors of Houses 1, 2, and 5.

The base of House 2's east wall remained in place; the rest had been broken and carried off by the mudflow.

the north, where nearly pure copper nodules were worked into highly valued sheets, or it might have drifted to Ozette from Japan as part of a ship's wreckage.

House 3, about two meters north of House 1, had been only partly blanketed by the mudflow that destroyed Houses 1 and 2, hence only part of it had been preserved. What remained suggested the house may have been abandoned, or was undergoing major repair, shortly before the mudflow struck. The side of a canoe evidently no longer seaworthy was serving as a wall plank, its gunwale still in place and replete with the wear marks left by paddles scraping against it. It seemed a signature of days spent fishing or sealing or whaling. Lying near it were a wooden feast dish carved to represent a seal and a small piece of sheet copper carefully wrapped in cedar bark. Stubs of three rafter-support posts broken off at floor level remained in place, covered with almost half a meter of clay. A fourth support post still lying on the floor impressed the archaeologists. It measured nearly six meters long, and Daugherty and Jeff Mauger (who had taken over as field director when Gleeson returned to Pullman to write his PhD dissertation) estimated its weight at about three-quarters of a ton. At that size, how did Ozette craftsmen produce it? Transport it? Erect it?

House 4 had been located but not excavated. The 1967 test pit dug uphill from the beach had indicated the likelihood of a house, and seven years later Daugherty and

Mauger decided to confirm its existence but not to excavate. Their decision owed partly to limited time and budget, and partly to archaeologists' ethic of leaving part of a site intact for future study when new excavation techniques and research questions are sure to have been developed. The strategy for House 4 was to confirm the presence of the planks recorded in the 1967 field notes and to test the immediate area for additional cultural evidence. This was done by trenching eastward from House 3. As anticipated, additional structural remains were encountered, including parts of a wall and the stub of a rafter-support post—enough to add House 4 to the roster of discoveries.

House 5 came as a surprise. It had been built on what at the time was a marshy, ill-chosen site, and perhaps for that reason it had soon been abandoned and partly salvaged. House 2 was later built on top of its remnants. Few artifacts remained in House 5, and overall workmanship suggested "a quick and dirty attitude toward construction," to quote Mauger's report, which mentioned, for example, that rafter support posts actually were not perpendicular to the house wall. "If the attitude evidenced toward questions of construction typified the head of household's attitude toward the maintenance of his other resources, the abandonment of the house may have come from the economic collapse of the household unit."

House 6, located in 1967, had stood to the south of House 1 and, judging by the stratigraphy, appeared to be contemporaneous with it. Time and funding ran out

A deep test pit revealed remnants of an older house underneath houses that had been excavated.

before it could be excavated. The mudflow that destroyed other houses apparently had washed through this house without leaving a thick clay deposit. House 6, therefore, could continue to be occupied but was destroyed by a different mudflow in early historic time.

House 7, also apparent in the stratigraphy of a test pit but not excavated, was close to House 6. It had been built early in the prehistoric time represented by Houses 1, 2, and 5, then abandoned for reasons that were not evident.

House 8, also not excavated, enticed the archaeology staff and crew. A deep test pit dug beneath the floor of House 2 exposed midden at a depth that was expected to reveal nothing but beach sand. However, as the July 24 camp log reports, "A lot of excitement and commotion. Found an artifact: pegged, zoomorphically flat carved wood." The next day's entry reads "15 more artifacts." And on the thirtieth the notation states simply: "Pit was filled in this A.M." Deteriorated whale bone, seal bones, poorly preserved shells, and wood fiber had come from the pit. Among the artifacts were a fishline weight, a bone or antler point, and six animal teeth, possibly once part of a necklace or pendant. There also was charcoal, important because it meant the deposit could be dated. In due time, Daugherty received word: 790 +/– 80 years B.P. (before present).

House 8 was twice the age of the other houses.

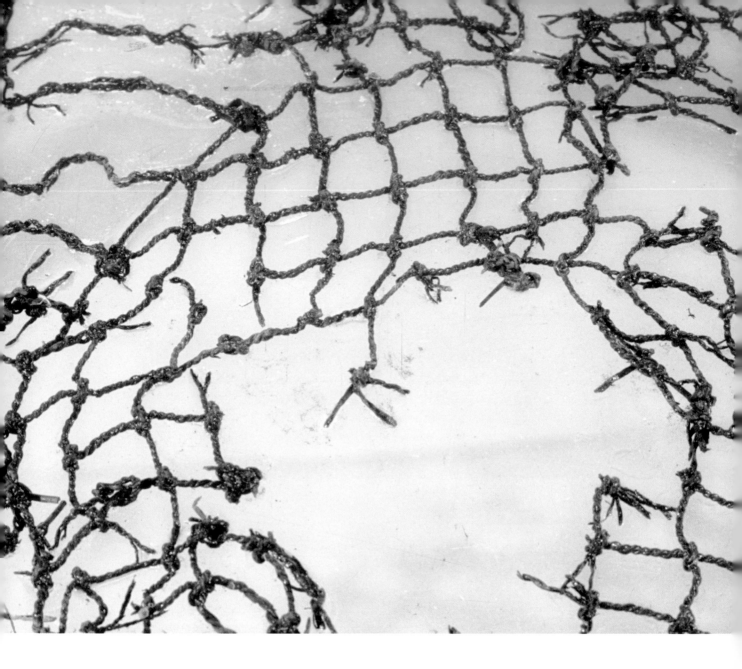

Netting from the excavation
at Ozette indicates aboriginal
fishing methods.

Chapter Four

Analysis

CLOSING THE EXCAVATION

THE CALENDAR HAD TURNED TO APRIL 1981 AND, AFTER ELEVEN YEARS, funding for work at Ozette was running out. Excavation ceased and archaeologists blanketed the remaining exposed portions of the excavation with sheets of plastic covered with mud so as to maintain the water saturated preservation of wooden objects still in the ground. Then they demolished their camp, cleaned up the debris, and departed. They had fully excavated three houses devastated by the mudflow and one partially so. They also had located four others. Significant parts of the standing houses had been swept away, but even so about 7,000 structural posts, poles, stakes, rafters, and planks were recovered, many of them broken by the impact of the mudflow. There also were more than a million shells and mammal, bird, and fish bones and about 55,000 wooden and fiber artifacts and pieces of artifacts, many of which could be reassembled. These included 1,200 box fragments, from which Jeff Mauger reassembled more than 50 whole boxes. Many of the remaining fragments were from boxes broken and discarded before the mudflow collapsed the houses. Similarly there were 112 wooden bowls and fragments of bowls, 324 canoe paddles and fragments, 1,160 wedges, 579 whetstones, 5,189 wooden arrow points, 103 bows, 110 harpoon shafts, and 629 halibut hooks and shanks. The numbers might have been even higher if the storage areas associated with benches along the west wall of House 1 had not been carried onto the beach by the mudflow.

For the Makahs, the nineteen pieces of fishnet were perhaps the most welcome artifacts to come from the excavation. Discovery of the first piece came in 1974, just as the Ninth Circuit Court, presided over by Judge George H. Boldt, was hearing a case intended to resolve conflicts between state fisheries officials and Indian tribes in regard to salmon. At issue in part was tribal use of nets, which the state contended was not the Makahs' practice aboriginally. But Ozette archaeology was about to vindicate oral tradition. Thinking back over the years of the dispute, tribal elder Hilary Irving remembered, "I kept telling them that we had been using nets for hundreds of years. It was just word-of-mouth history, but I knew from my forefathers. . . . I kept telling people and telling people, and then this one day I come home from a fisheries meeting and the first person I see is Ed Claplanhoo. And he said, 'You know what they found down at Ozette?' and I said, 'No. What did they find now?' And he said 'A piece of net!' So I got to say, 'I told you so.' My people used nets long before any white men came around." For the Makahs, there is no question but that the Ozette evidence influenced Judge Boldt's decision. He ruled that the 1855 treaties guaranteed Indians' right to continue fishing as they always had. Tribes and the state are to comanage the fish.

Funding ran out, excavation ceased, and the archaeology camp was burned to let vegetation regrow.

In Neah Bay, the laboratory remained busy as the end of the Ozette project loomed. Makah tribal members had worked both at the excavation site and in the lab; and as planned from the beginning, they were ready to take over the preservation, storage, and display of the Ozette material. A successful treatment for some of the "problem" hardwood artifacts had been found. Grosso first soaked them in acetone, which replaced the water in the wood. Then he put them into a saturated rosin-acetone solution, in which they were held for ninety days at 120 degrees Fahrenheit. This forced the rosin into the wood. Next, he let the acetone evaporate, leaving the rosin to stabilize the wood. Other artifacts presented different problems. A surface film of Carbowax persisted in marring the appearance of certain objects. Ethanol seemed to be an answer, but it was effective only until high atmospheric humidity drew the Carbowax that had soaked into the wood back to the surface. The technique could be valuable only for artifacts displayed or stored in a low-humidity environment.

For Professor Daugherty and the graduate students working with him, ending work at the excavation site meant that no new studies could be undertaken—no investigation of the eight-hundred-year-old house deep below House 2, and no funds for determining additional dates on any of the houses that had been excavated. However, analysis of everything that had already been found could continue. Ozette was unique in the opportunity it gave to study routine household life suddenly stopped

Ozette Research

The following scholarly reports were developed during the active phase of the Ozette Project; additional studies of the archaeological collection continue to be made.

Croes, Dale R. 1973. "An Analysis of Prehistoric Baskets from the Ozette Site, Cape Alava." Master's thesis, Department of Archaeology, WSU.

————. 1975. "Basketry from the Ozette Village Archaeological Site: A Technological, Functional, and Comparative Study." PhD diss., Department of Archaeology, WSU.

DePuydt, Raymond T. 1983. "Cultural Implications of Avifaunal Remains Recovered from the Ozette Site." Master's thesis, Department of Archaeology, WSU.

Draper, John. 1989. "Lithic Analysis." Master's thesis, Department of Archaeology, WSU.

Ellison, Jeffrey A. 1977. "The Ozette Petroglyphs." Master's thesis, Department of Archaeology, WSU.

Friedman, Edward I. 1976. "An Archaeological Survey of Makah Territory: A Study in Resource Utilization." PhD diss., Department of Archaeology, WSU.

Friedman, Janet P. 1975. "The Prehistoric Uses of Wood at the Ozette Archaeological Site." PhD diss., Department of Archaeology, WSU.

Gill, Steven J. 1983. "Ethnobotany of the Makah and Ozette People, Olympic Peninsula, Washington." PhD diss., Department of Botany, WSU.

Gleeson, Paul F., Jr. 1970. "Dog Remains from the Ozette Village Archaeological Site." Master's thesis, Department of Archaeology, WSU.

————. 1980. "Ozette Woodworking Technology." PhD diss., Department of Archaeology, WSU.

Huelsbeck, David R. 1980. "Utilization of Fish at the Ozette Site." Master's thesis, Department of Archaeology, WSU.

————. 1983. "Mammals and Fish in the Subsistence Economy of Ozette." PhD diss., Department of Archaeology, WSU.

Kent, Susan. 1975. "An Analysis of Northwest Coast Combs with Special Emphasis on Those from Ozette." Master's thesis, Department of Archaeology, WSU.

Koch, Jennifer L. 1975. "Miniatures from the Archaeological Inventory at the Ozette Village Site." Master's thesis, Department of Archaeology, WSU.

Mauger, Jeffrey E. 1978. "Shed Roof Houses at the Ozette Archaeological Site:

A Protohistoric Architectural System." PhD diss., Department of Archaeology, WSU.

McKenzie, Kathleen H. 1974. "Ozette Prehistory Prelude." Master's thesis, Department of Archaeology, University of Calgary.

Samuels, Stephan R. 1977. "Investigations into Computer Graphics: Archaeological Applications." Master's thesis, Department of Archaeology, WSU.

———. 1982. "Spatial Patterns and Cultural Processes in Three Northwest Coast Longhouse Floor Middens from Ozette." PhD diss., Department of Archaeology, WSU.

Wessen, Gary C. 1982. "Shell Middens as Cultural Deposits: A Case Study from Ozette." PhD diss., Department of Archaeology, WSU.

Richard Daugherty listened to plans for closing the excavation.

by catastrophe. Here were actual houses with their contents intact. Understanding them called for first gathering as much data as possible, then making sense of it. An extraordinary nine PhD dissertations and ten master's theses would come from the one project.

THE FAUNAL REMAINS

The sheer volume of Ozette faunal remains posed a challenge. Mammal bones and fragments of bones numbered 260,000, bird bones 10,000, fish bones 600,000, and shellfish remains 400,000 to 500,000. All had to be identified, coded, and entered into a computer. At the time, computers were a new technology, one of immense value in comparing and interpreting various types of data. Ethnographic and historic records also had to be searched and Makah elders interviewed. It was a huge undertaking.

First the faunal remains had to be sorted and identified, a tedious process of matching bones and shells from the archaeological deposits with counterparts in established, already-identified collections. In Pullman, as one student commented, "practically every anthropology major in the WSU work-study program" sorted material caught in the mesh that screened runoff from the excavation squares. At Ozette on days when the notoriously stormy wet weather precluded excavating, winter crews joined PhD candidates David Huelsbeck and Gary Wessen in patiently identifying mammal bones and shellfish remains. In Neah Bay, Edward Friedman sorted mammal bones, other than those of whales, which were easily recognizable by size alone. He undertook assembling a comparative collection of bones from land and sea mammals native to the Ozette area. Archaeologists at the excavation site collected local specimens and sent them by helicopter to Neah Bay. Friedman, his wife, Janet, and their two young sons walked various beaches, adding to the collection, and trappers and landowners in the area brought dead animals to him and reported where to find roadkills. Friedman's task was to salvage the bones—not a simple undertaking.

For several reasons Friedman decided against using the Dermestes beetles, relatives of carpet beetles, which are often used to deflesh bones: they must be maintained at eighty to eighty-five degrees Fahrenheit and less than 60 percent humidity, conditions scarcely characteristic of the Neah Bay climate, and they are costly. Instead, Friedman put carcasses in metal containers with holes drilled into them, then suspended the containers from a local pier and waited for small marine arthropods to eat the flesh. This did not work out well. Storm surges broke the lines tethering the containers—whether rope lines or steel cables—and the arthropods expected to feed on the flesh gave only "irregular service." To better control the environment, Friedman tried establishing a colony of the arthropods in one of the laboratory tanks used for preserving artifacts, but the effort failed. Thinking that the high oil content in raw sea-mammal flesh might be distasteful to the arthropods, he tried boiling the carcasses before placing them back in the bay, with the metal containers secured more firmly to the piers. That worked. The comparative collection was complete enough for species identification to begin.

Excavated bones included a few from bears and river otters, along with even fewer from beavers, minks, weasels, mice, red squirrels, martens, and skunks. Most of these small species had little food value and no useable bone. They were essentially missing from House 1 but common in House 2, its less wealthy neighbor. In all houses, deer

At least ethnographically, hats identified wearers by class: knobbed for the highest rank, flat-topped for commoners and slaves.

seemed the most hunted land mammal, followed by elk. At least that was true according to the bone count. But the count may be misleading. Hunters most likely dressed deer and elk at kill sites rather than carry home whole carcasses; the presence of a few bones may actually represent several animals. Similarly, butchering seals and whales and cleaning fish on the village beach would let the tide do the cleanup, and none of those bones would be represented in the middens.

A total of eighteen species of fish were present in the inside and outside middens of the buried houses, but they were not evenly distributed. House 1 fish bones were concentrated in the corner evidently occupied by a whaler's family. It may be that feasts held in this wealthy part of the house explain this exceptional fish-bone concentration; it was where archaeologists had found the wall panel with a carving of a whale, baskets holding whale harpoon blades, a knobbed hat, and exotic, high-value shells. Most of the fish bones were from choice species. For example, there were three times as many halibut bones in House 1 as in House 2, occupied by families that apparently had access to only relatively poor fishing areas. House 1 families must have owned the most highly productive halibut banks, such as those north of Cape Flattery today.

The discarded shells of eighty-nine marine invertebrate species had collected in and around the houses. Wessen calculated that they represented about four thousand kilograms (4.5 tons) of meat, more than would suggest the so-called starvation diet often mentioned ethnographically, yet constituting only 10 to 20 percent of the total diet. Aside from food, the shellfish also provided fish bait, medicines, and raw material for tools, implements, and decorative items. Furthermore, the occupants of House 1 specialized in prime shellfish species such as butter clams, littlenecks, blue mussels, California mussels, and periwinkles. In House 2, remains of these species were comparatively few but there were abundant remnants of inferior food species such as chitons, limpets, and urchins. Wessen reasoned that collecting areas for shellfish must have been owned and managed by individual family headmen, as seemed true for fishing areas. He also cautioned, however, that "the evidence of food resources recovered at Ozette, or any archaeological site, is exactly that—the evidence of food resources recovered." This is not the same as deducing what the villagers ate; some types of food residue are more likely to preserve well than others, and cultural factors such as when the food was processed and how often the floor was swept also enter the equation. Wessen could record and analyze only the shellfish processed in and around the houses. There was no way to know about what was processed or eaten elsewhere. However, from shell growth rings (much like trees' growth rings), he could infer the season of harvest, and they indicated that at least part of the Ozette village must have been lived in year-round.

Bones of forty-two species of birds were represented by faunal remains, most

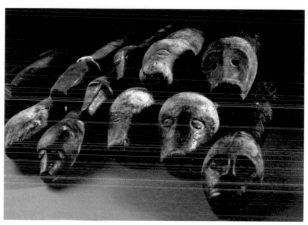

For hundreds of years, fur seals were the chief prey of Ozette hunters. Later they became a major Euro-American trade item: their fleece has an astonishing three hundred thousand fibers per square inch.

Heavy wooden clubs, used to stun and kill harpooned seals, seem unique to Ozette; such clubs are unknown elsewhere.

of them seabirds probably taken by seal hunters and whalers while offshore pursuing their main prey. One basket, stored inside a larger basket, held nothing but gull wing bones, and Raymond DePuydt, studying the cultural implications of avifaunal remains for his master's thesis, concluded that birds may have been valued for their bones and feathers as much as for food. Two-thirds of Ozette's bird-bone tools came from albatross and gull bone, followed in frequency by pelican and cormorant bone. Uses for the bone ranged from simple awls beveled to a point at one end to composite fishhooks with bird-bone points attached to wooden shanks. Birds also provided feathers to decorate dance costumes and, stripped of their quills, to mix with dog wool for blankets.

Ninety-five percent of the Ozette mammal bones were from marine species, and northern fur seals accounted for 90 percent of that 95 percent. Porpoises, sea lions, and sea otters followed next in abundance, but the ratio of these three to the seals was about one to twenty-five. Fundamentally an oceanic species, the fur seals came—and still come—close to shore at Ozette. Females follow along the edge of the continental shelf when migrating to Alaska to breed in spring and again in fall when returning south with their pups. That route puts them more than thirty miles offshore except in the Ozette area, where the shelf is only about twelve miles offshore. Testing a variety of sites in traditional Makah territory for his PhD research, Edward Friedman and his Makah assistant, Kirk Wachendorf, consistently found that "the only mammal occurring in large numbers is the northern fur seal." Furthermore, this held true through time. The prevalence of fur seal bones in the 1966 excavation trench made it clear that sea hunters had paddled out from Ozette after seals for more than a thousand years, and at Hoko (along the Strait of Juan de Fuca east of Neah Bay) fur seal bones dominated mammal remains in a thousand-year-old rock shelter. Indeed, the bones have been abundant for the last five thousand years at various archaeological sites from Southern California to the eastern Aleutians.

Master's-degree candidate Marian Fisken studied whale skeletons at Yale University's Peabody Museum, the Smithsonian Institution, the Whaling Museum in New Bedford, Massachusetts, and the Boston aquarium. She and Huelsbeck then set to work identifying and analyzing the 3,402 Ozette whale bones. By far, most of the bones were from gray and humpback whales, species that swim slowly and come fairly close to shore. Both migrate north in spring, south in late fall, and most likely some remained along the Washington coast through the summer. There also were a few bones from right whales and finback whales and from one blue whale. Several whale vertebrae, scapulae, and maxilla (jaw bones) had the tips of mussel-shell harpoon blades broken off in them. Interestingly, out of ten such humpback scapulae with remnant blade tips, three had been penetrated from the whale's right side. This contradicts ethnographic reports of whalers always approaching their quarry from the left.

Whales provided meat, blubber, oil, bone, and sinew. Inner bone is porous, but outer bone as much as four centimeters thick is compact and strong. By cutting parallel grooves and then prying, craftsmen could obtain pieces of bone ten to thirty-five centimeters long, ample for making into a variety of tools. The Ozette inventory includes seventy-one whale-bone wedges, fifty-six bark shredders, thirteen adze handles, eight bark beaters, five spindle whorls, and one mat creaser. There also are whale-bone clubs for use as weapons, and whale-bone digging sticks for unearthing roots to eat and to use in making baskets. There are even bones that served as cutting boards. Most of these are left ulnae (one of the three major fin bones), and this led Fisken and Huelsbeck to wonder why they were preferred to right ulnae. Maybe it was because, as a person's work progressed, a left ulna's natural curve brought addi-

Cordage ranged from withes to ropes. *Left:* Cedar-bough withe with a sheetbend knot, probably part of a sling used for holding house wall planks in place. Sheetbends could be easily untied to remove planks for reuse at seasonal resource camps, such as those on Tatoosh Island and at the Ozette River. *Right:* Heavy-gauge cedar-bough rope used as a whaling harpoon line. The running noose at the end probably permitted attachment of a sealskin float to buoy a harpooned whale.

tional useable surface areas within easy reach. Conversely, the curve of a right ulna would put useable surfaces increasingly out of reach. Humpback whale ulnae seemed preferred to those of gray whales; they are flatter. For tools, however, just the opposite was true. Humpback radii (another of the major fin bones) seemed preferable to gray whale radii; they are straighter and their outer bone is smoother, heavier, and harder.

Whale bones were also valued for use in construction. They diverted runoff, covered drainage trenches crossing house floors, gave structure to the community drainage ditch outside House 1, and were interlocked to form retaining walls resistant to downslope creep. They also held fill in place when space for a new house was leveled, and they provided bulkhead protection along the village sea bank.

CORDAGE AND BASKETRY

Cordage—string and rope—draws little attention yet was crucial to Northwest Coast culture. For example, without rope, a whaler could not retrieve his harpoon, and without a collar of cordage around its top, a wooden wedge would split when pounded and so would quickly become useless.

For PhD candidate Dale Croes, Ozette cordage and basketry became the focus of research. He defined cordage as "any rope, cord, or string that is twisted, braided, or a plain strip of bark, limb, twig, or root." In the Ozette collection, he found more than 2,000 examples. Of them, 530 have knots, which Croes defined as "any intertwining, looping, bending, hitching, folding, or gathering together of one or more pieces of cordage in such a way as to produce a tying together, fastening, binding, or connecting of the length on, to, or with itself [or] another length. . . . Any cordage arrangement that meets these criteria is considered a knot—unless it's a tangle!"

Withes were the simplest form of cordage—tough, flexible boughs and twigs. They held house wallboards in place and sewed bow and stern pieces onto canoes. Their knots were almost all sheetbends, a strong knot that can be easily untied. More elaborate than withes were red-cedar boughs twisted

Makah women continue to make baskets, which they regard as a major link with the past. Pictured here is the late Isabell Ides, master Makah basket-maker.

and used either singly or made into multistrand rope. Quileute elder Bill Penn, age ninety-two at the time and living in Neah Bay, told Croes that the first step in making cedar rope was to peel bark from the boughs of young trees, then push each bough into the hollow stem of bull kelp. Next, the kelp tubes would be laid on the beach side by side, covered with sand, and a fire would be built on top. The fire had to be tended until the boughs had softened. Then they could be pulled out of the kelp and twisted into rope.

Strips of bark from red cedar trees furnished the raw material for Ozette's most common cordage, typically made by braiding. Also common were spruce roots twisted into multistrand cords to furnish fishline leaders on halibut hooks and to make into nets. Strips of wild-cherry bark formed a third major type of cordage. It bound barbs onto fishhooks and harpoon blades, attached points and fletching onto arrow shafts, and formed hand grips on bows. Like rawhide, cherry bark tightens as it dries.

When Croes began his analysis of basketry, Makah women not only *invited* him to join their classes at Neah Bay schools, they *insisted* that he attend. They also impressed upon him that basketry is rich with carefully safeguarded traditions. Although his fingers would learn to weave and his mind would know the merit of various materials, he was never to teach basketry himself or to sell anything he made. Thus culturally prepared, he began his study.

More than five hundred basketry items had come from House 1 alone. Most were found where their owners had kept them, and many still held their original contents.

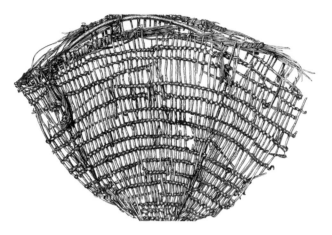

A large, twined pack basket would have been used for carrying everything from clams and fish to firewood. Its open weave let water drain out.

Cedar-root baskets made by coiling rather than twining came from the buried houses. They are typical of Salish baskets, not Makah.

There were sturdy baskets for carrying and storage, small baskets to use when picking berries, and four styles of hats. There were mats of cedar bark and of bulrush for multipurpose use as mattresses, insulating liners for walls, space dividers defining individual family living areas, and covers for beached canoes. There were the two large, flat bags holding whale harpoon blades and smaller flat bags with fishing tackle. There were some baskets made in the Salish way by coiling rather than twining, an "imported" style that could have been acquired in trade or through potlatching, or made at Ozette by Salish women who married in or were brought as slaves. There were basketry cradles and infant face covers, possibly an indication of high rank. There were even mudshoes, thought by Makah elders to be similar in function to snowshoes, but for use in marshy areas.

In all, fifty-six types of baskets came from in and around House 1, and by plotting where each was found Croes corroborated ethnographic reports of each nuclear family keeping its own tools and implements and its own supplies of raw materials and food. On and behind benches in the houses, archaeologists found large storage baskets with rolled bundles of cedar bark, weavers' kits, and bags full of cattail heads, bird feathers, paint pigments, awls, fishhooks, knives, and whetstones. They also found empty storage baskets with broken rims and handles. Probably these once had been filled with dried food and hung high on the wall or a support post where smoke drifting around the ceiling area would help preserve the contents. Only one basket was found away from the corners. Large and sturdy, it remained in the central floor area, where families cooked their meals on individual hearths. In it were a dozen cobbles from the beach, apparently ready for use in a hearth or to cook food by first heating the cobbles in a fire, then dropping them into a box filled with water.

Such stones were part of research done by graduate students Allan Stanfill and John Draper on Ozette lithics. Termed "fire-modified rock," they are an archaeologi-

cal marker of human activity recognized worldwide, and the men's goal was to determine whether rocks that had only been heated in a fire could be distinguished from those that were first heated, then suddenly cooled by being plunged into the water of a cooking box. They made their test by placing fist-size basalt and sandstone cobbles from the beach at various distances from a fire and leaving them for various lengths of time. Predictably, the cobbles spalled as their outer surface expanded more rapidly than the interior. That type of breakage resulted only from direct heating in a fire. In contrast, cobbles from a cooking box broke into jagged fragments. Thus, from shattered rock an archaeologist can infer cooking methods: human behavior revealed by a stone.

To make a box, Jeff Mauger first steamed a kerfed board over wet seaweed resting on hot coals. Next he bent the board at the kerfs to form the sides of the box. His final steps would be to close the corner with pegs and then peg on a bottom piece.

WOOD TECHNOLOGY

By microscopic examination of cell structure, Janet Friedman identified the kinds of wood in regular use at Ozette, each selected for its particular physical properties. Red cedar, of course, was one of these woods. The huge size of the trees and the wood's straight grain and ease of splitting made it ideal for house planks and for canoes. Another advantage of cedar is its durability owing to its high resin content, which is toxic to fungi and insects. Furthermore, it can be bent when heated while wet. A newly made dugout canoe was widened by filling it with water and hot rocks to soften the wood, then inserting thwarts. Similarly, a board that was kerfed at three places could be steamed and bent to form the sides of a box: *hax-wi-duk-sh*, the Makah word for "box" means "folded together."

But using red cedar was only part of Ozette wood technology. All the intact whaling harpoon shafts and fragments of shafts excavated at Ozette are yew. It is a heavy

Boxes came in all sizes, some plain, some elaborately carved, such as this unfinished box front (*right*) measuring twenty-three centimeters by thirteen centimeters, found on the floor of House 2. Notice the pegs at the left corner and bottom of the box.

wood, and that weight added force to a harpoon blade's penetration of a whale's tough skin. Harpoons for whales were thrust, not thrown, the opposite of sealing harpoons which were thrown and therefore had shafts made from a lighter wood. Clubs for stunning and killing seals after they were harpooned, however, had to be heavy—and thirty-one out of the thirty-five seal clubs found at Ozette are yew. The other four are crab apple, which is also a heavy wood but tends to crack and split and therefore, to quote Friedman, "is unlikely to hold up under the abuse of repeated use."

Sticks like those used at Ozette are still used for roasting salmon.

The physical attributes of yew made it also right for bows. Subject to pulling at each end, bows simultaneously need tensile strength on the outer (convex) side and compressive strength on the inner (concave) side. In addition, the wood must resist the sudden shock of an arrow's release, then the return of stress as the bowstring is again drawn taut. Of thirty full-sized bows at Ozette, twenty-seven are yew. There also are eleven small bows, presumably for boys to play with. These were made of various woods, including salmonberry, dogwood, Indian plum, and red cedar, all of which were more readily available than yew and easier to work. Arrow points were not flaked from stone but made of straight pieces of bone or wood. Of five hundred wooden points, almost three hundred were Sitka spruce, and more than one hundred were western hemlock. Both woods are stiff enough to penetrate prey without bending or breaking. Both are also easily carved and locally available, essential qualities considering how many arrows were needed.

Like arrow points, halibut hooks needed a stiff, strong wood. That suggests another use for spruce, but it is resinous and seems to have been distasteful to halibut. Of 182 halibut hooks at Ozette, 109 were hemlock, 69 fir, and only four spruce. Conversely, spruce was favored for wedges, although ethnographic reports have said they were made of yew in order to withstand pounding. Not so at Ozette. There, most wedges were made from spruce compression wood, the unique, strong-grained wood that forms on the stressed underside of a branch or leaning trunk.

Friedman found the range of woods used by Ozette craftsmen, and their finesse in selecting each one, to be remarkable. Even relatively minor objects warranted attention to the attributes of specific woods. Red alder and bigleaf maple carve easily and have no odor; they were ideal for bowls and platters that held food. Combs need elastic strength to avoid breaking, and dogwood, redberry elder, cascara, salal, and yew were all suitable. Of four sticks found at Ozette for holding salmon close to a fire to roast, three are Douglas-fir and one is red cedar. Both these woods are straight grained and will split readily; both are stiff enough to hold the weight of the cooking fish. A difference is that the Douglas-fir has no taste, whereas the cedar does. Even so, Makah women today use cedar sticks to hold their fish, and they were surprised to learn that Douglas-fir had ever been used.

TOOLS

Woodworkers were also remarkable toolmakers. Paul Gleeson categorized, analyzed, and described 2,444 Ozette tools, nearly all for woodworking. There were seven basic types—adzes, drills, knives, chisels, abraders, wedges, and mauls—and they were made from one of five kinds of raw material: bone, tooth, stone, shell, and metal. Handles were wood or bone.

The same care that went into selecting certain kinds of wood for certain uses also went into selecting materials for tools. Whale rib bone added weight to adze handles and thereby increased the effectiveness of blades. Beaver incisors served as a type of blade, their natural curve an asset in producing decorative effects. The edges of cobble spalls could easily be sharpened and the spalls hafted to make effective tools, but

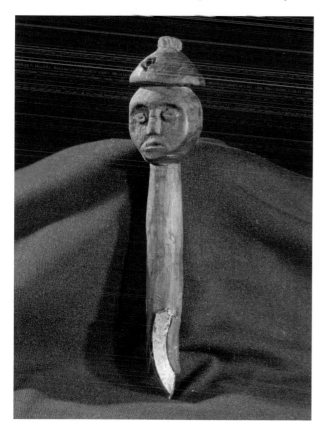

Beaver incisors made effective blades for woodworking tools.

cobbles also were laboriously pecked into mauls to use for tapping chisels or gouges, or for pounding wedges to split wood. Five intact mauls and pieces of six others were found at Ozette. Hours had gone into making each one, but few were needed. That contrasts with the 789 sandstone whetstones that came from Ozette! Whetstones must have been constantly needed to keep tool edges sharp, and fortunately they would have come from the beach virtually ready-made and even ranging in grit size, from coarse to fine.

By far the main material for sharp-edged tools was the shell of the California mussel, from the outer reef at Ozette. More than seven hundred shell knives, harpoon points, and fragments of knives and points came from the excavations. At least three hundred of these were complete, a significant number when compared with the fewer than four hundred such implements known archaeologically for the entire Northwest Coast. The high number at Ozette owes partly to extraordinary preservation conditions, partly to the extensive excavation of the site, and partly to the use of water as an excavation tool—a gentle way to free even small and

mundane objects from the mud that obscured them. Gleeson found it took only fifteen minutes to make a shell knife sharp enough to cut wood or flesh, and pouches holding mussel shells and whetstones were an almost standard part of the Ozette tool inventory. Thus equipped, a seal hunter or a woodworker, or a woman preparing dinner, could quickly resharpen or replace a knife, and Gleeson concluded that for House 1 the effective working life of the hundreds of ground-shell blades about equaled that of the twenty-eight metal blades. Shell blades were quick and easy to make. Metal blades were durable.

How Ozette toolmakers worked iron or steel into their style of blades remained little more than speculation. No blades indicated Japanese or other foreign manufacture; Ozette craftsmen must have worked—or reworked—the metal themselves. The curved cutting edge of Ozette chisel blades, for example, could only result from having been hammered into shape and then sharpened. Probably the metal was not cold hammered; that would produce cracks. The toolmakers must have learned to use heating and cooling techniques to alter the metal's hardness and therefore its ability to stay sharp. Most likely, the metal washed ashore embedded in wreckage that drifted across the Pacific. Or maybe shipwreck survivors who occasionally drifted into Ozette territory had knowledge of working metal and

Present-day carver Greg Colfax has marveled at the skill of his Ozette predecessors, pointing out that whoever carved this box front knew how to maintain the sharpness of a blade as well as can be done today. The box front measures seventy-eight centimeters by fifty-one centimeters.

shared it with their captors. This is known among Chinook people at the mouth of the Columbia River.

HOUSE ARCHITECTURE

In his dissertation on Ozette architecture, Jeff Mauger identified seven wooden structural elements—planks, posts, poles, beams, stakes and pegs, and withes—and three nonwooden. The latter three were rock roof-weights, rock posthole linings, and whale bones.

Large logs lying on the forest floor and drift logs lying on the beach were valuable; Makah elder Ty Parker told Mauger that old men would pass the time looking out to sea, watching for floating logs and promptly claiming each one even before it washed ashore. According to ethnographic reports, men also cut down standing trees. They first chiseled notches into the trunk and then split out the wood between the notches, a "gnawing" process that continued until they could pry out a slab or fell the entire tree. Using wedges and mauls they split the log into planks, some of them as much as one and a half meters wide and measuring two to five meters long.

To some extent the men must have anticipated a plank's intended use as they worked. Bench planks had to be not only wide but also able to bear considerable weight; they averaged four to six centimeters thick, more than planks for the walls of a house, which needed to be lightweight and therefore relatively easy to handle. However, some roof planks were split out thick. That allowed for subsequent adzing to form a raised "lip" along the edge of one surface or, in a few cases, both edges. Or sometimes the lips were formed by carving out the center of the planks, leaving the

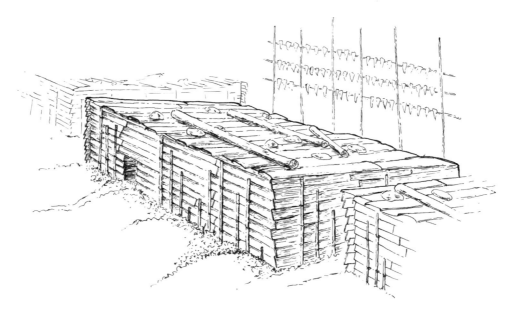

Ozette architecture could be discerned from structural remains preserved by the mudflow and complete even to fish-drying racks along the rear wall.

Immense timbers notched at the top were designed to support rafter beams. They were set into the earthen floor of a house, as much as a meter deep, and shimmed in place with rocks.

original thickness at the edges, or they were formed by simply carving gutters near each edge of a thick plank. The lipped planks were laid alternately, one with lipped side up, the next with lipped side down. This interlocked the boards and formed a roof that fairly effectively shed rain.

Sturdy upright posts supported rafter beams that crossed the house interior from one long wall to the other. How the posts were placed determined the width of a house. Length depended on how far apart the posts stood and how many of them there were. House 2 (ten meters wide by seventeen meters long) had four pairs of posts. House 1 (ten meters wide by twenty meters long) had been built with five pairs but only one lone post along the front (west) wall remained. The mudflow may have swept away the others; they may have later eroded onto the beach; or they may have been salvaged for reuse elsewhere. Roofs sloped front to back, their angle determined by the differing heights of the support posts along the front and back walls. Mauger estimated that the east (back) wall of House 1 had been about three meters high. The west wall, demolished and carried away by the mudflow, quite surely stood higher.

The first step in building a house was erecting support posts for the rafter beams, which rested in a U-shaped notch at the top of each post. Deep holes lined with rocks kept the posts upright. Rafters ran the length of the house, and roof planks were laid onto them, then rocks weighted the planks in place. Thus, the house framework was complete in itself. It stood independent of the walls, which were made by sand-wiching planks between pairs of close-set poles. Each successive row of wall planks overlapped the outside of the row below it, thereby as much as possible keeping rain from blowing in. Withes tied the planks in place. The doorway of House 1 apparently was near the middle of the west wall. The same was true for House 2, although there also was some evidence of a north entry.

Overhead, Ozette houses apparently had none of the rafter storage features known ethnographically and historically in traditional Makah houses. If such storage existed at Ozette, its constituent poles and planks and ropes might well have been impossible to recognize amid the wreckage created by the mudflow. On the other hand, poles to support fish-drying racks lay along the exterior east wall of House 1. A sharply pointed base eased the setting of such posts upright, and they were fitted with crosspieces to hold the fish. For secure support, poles evidently were tied to a house wall with withes.

Nothing at Ozette indicated the use of floor planks. Flooring was simply the accu-mulation of midden—wood chips, hearths, fire-cracked rocks, animal bones, and scores of wooden stakes and pegs of various sizes, their purpose(s) indiscernible. The floor in House 1 ranged from twenty to forty centimeters thick and was finely layered, owing to decades of trampling and sweeping. While excavating, archaeol-ogists could adjust the pressure and volume of spray from their hoses and thereby trace individual floor deposits. This let them recognize "pathways" both inside and outside of the house, a discernment that would have been impossible if excavating with shovels and trowels. As it was, the spray made heavy traffic areas in the center of the house stand out clearly from lesser traffic areas. They were free of rock and bones and anything else that would be "unfriendly to bare feet," as Gleeson expressed it. Seemingly, extra sweeping and cleaning went on there.

Bench planks lined interior walls resting on stakes driven into the floor. They were set only twenty to thirty centimeters above the floor and, along with planks on the floor in front of them, they served as places to lounge, work, and sleep. Rows of close-set snail opercula decorated the front edge of one bench in House 1, an indication of wealth. Cut marks, punctures, and scratches in the wood of all benches hinted at the work that had taken place on them, which ranged from food preparation, to process-ing raw materials, to manufacturing tools and hunting gear.

HOW OLD?

Dating the houses proved difficult, although Dr. Daugherty and his team of graduate students could say with confidence that the houses struck by the mudflow predate Euro-American influence. No objects of foreign origin lay within them other than the

Japanese metal that had drifted across the Pacific; the era of contact and trade with outsiders had not yet begun, although it would soon do so. The houses are prehistoric. Two methods of determining age—radioactive-carbon dating (C-14) and dendrochronology (tree-ring dating)—have given dates, although both have limitations. A third possible indication of age links the disastrous Ozette mudflow to a dated earthquake.

The radioactive-carbon method dated charcoal from a hearth in House 1, determining that it was 440 years old, plus or minus 90 years. This does not represent when the house was built or when the mudflow struck. It relates to the age of the wood burned in the hearth but not necessarily to when it burned. This dating method is possible owing to a complex series of events. All organisms require carbon. Plants absorb it from the atmosphere through photosynthesis; herbivorous animals get it from the plants they eat; and carnivores get it by eating herbivores. In a living organism, for every trillion stable atoms of carbon (C-12) there will be one atom that is radioactive and unstable (C-14). When the organism dies, the C-14 in its tissues continues to decay and is not replaced. This changes the ratio of C-14 to C-12. Half of the C-14 will be gone in 5,730 years, half of the remaining C-14 in another 5,730 years, and so on. The method works well for dating samples that are 40,000 to 50,000 years old or older. It does not work as well for samples 500 or fewer years old. This is true because the possible measurement error, indicated by the standard deviation—the plus/minus figure—is too great.

The C-14 dating method has been used by archaeologists worldwide ever since its development in 1949 by Willard Libby, at the time a chemist at the University of Chicago. However, it now is realized that the amount of C-14 in the atmosphere—and therefore in an organism—fluctuates rather than holding steady as had been assumed. This is because sun-spot cycles and Earth's magnetic field affect the cosmic radiation that produces the atmospheric C-14, and they do not hold steady. Furthermore, the "B.P." following a C-14 date means "Before Present," but that "present" means 1950, when laboratories began using Libby's method. Radiocarbon years might better be written, some scientists suggest, not as "B.P." but as "C-14 years before 1950." Better yet, standardized tables now recalibrate radiocarbon years into calendar years. The relationship between the two is complicated, not linear.

Human behavior also has affected the accuracy of the C-14 method. About 150 years ago, the Industrial Revolution started adding to the atmosphere very old carbon from coal, oil, and gas; and atom-bomb tests in the 1960s more than doubled the amount of atmospheric radioactive carbon (much of it now absorbed by the world's oceans). Further problems may come from the presumed relation of a test sample to the surface it lies on. A burrowing rodent may have displaced it, or erosion may have jumbled the associated strata, or ground seepage may have contaminated it with carbon older than the sample's true age. Human judgment in selecting and handling

Charcoal from a floor hearth provided a C-14 date.

samples is crucial—and even then there may be problems. For example, the charcoal in an Ozette hearth could be from fairly fresh twigs and branches, the center of centuries-old tree trunks, or driftwood washed downriver from a distant forest and tossed onto the beach by waves. Even so, the 440+/–90 B.P. date is reasonable, and converting it to calendar years indicates that House 1 was occupied sometime between 1310 and 1640.

Dendrochronology provides dates equivalent to calendar dates. The method is based on counting annual growth rings formed in the cambium of trees, the layer just under the bark. The rings' width will vary from year to year and tree to tree, even in the same species living in the same region, but the pattern of thicker rings in favorable years and thinner ones in unfavorable years will be the same from tree to tree. The outermost ring will represent the last year of the tree's life and earlier dates can be determined by counting back from it toward the center of the trunk. The technique was developed in the early 1900s in the arid Southwest, but it was not until the 1970s that dendrochronology work began in the moist climate of the coastal Northwest—and ran into complications. Seasonal growth is less distinct in the Northwest than in the Southwest. Trees that grow well one year tend to carry over excess nutrients from that year to the next, and consequently their ring patterns may differ considerably from those of nearby trees. Furthermore, the huge size of Northwest trees makes it impossible to core to the center of a trunk for a complete set of rings. Also, surface and near-surface wood tends to decay rapidly and thereby eliminate the rings that indicate the last years of a tree's life. For these reasons establishing a master tree-ring set is difficult.

Nonetheless, in the late 1970s two dendrochronology dates were obtained at Ozette. At the time, Northwest dendro studies were little more than beginning, and crucial computer software was unavailable to aid in matching tree-ring mea-

Hundreds of stakes had been set into the house floors, most of them enigmatic. They still could be dated. Here Paul Gleeson contemplates the angle at which these are bent, indication of the direction and force of the mudflow.

surements. However, two planks from House 1 were dated. Growth rings in one of them indicated the tree it came from was still living in 1613, and those of the other in 1719. How much later the planks actually became part of the house cannot be known, because neither plank had its crucial outermost growth ring. The dates merely establish that one tree was still living in 1613, the other in 1719. How many growth rings were lost when the planks were made is unknown. Furthermore, written records indicate that planks were labor-intensive to produce and often were moved from place to place. Thus, an old plank might be used in building a new house; its date would apply only to that particular plank, not to the whole house.

For any of these reasons, the dendrochronology dates from Ozette are not definitive, although they roughly fit the few other dates available. More dendro dates still could be obtained. It is reasonable to assume that the posts and stakes in the buried houses were put to use soon after cutting. If so, their outer rings would still be intact—and there are hundreds of these posts and stakes now curated at Neah Bay, many with the bark still on. They could be dated.

A third possible source for dating the burial of houses at Ozette is a violent earthquake that shook the Northwest Coast from southern British Columbia to Northern California. Quakes commonly trigger landslides, and documented evidence of this quake includes quicksand-filled cracks along the Columbia River and slide deposits on the floor of a Vancouver Island fjord near Port Alberni. The shaking may also have caused the slope behind part of the Ozette village to give way as a massive mudflow.

ANALYSIS

Effects of this exceedingly violent earthquake helped solve a puzzle along the southern coast of Washington and may have implications for Ozette. For decades archaeologists found relatively little evidence of prehistoric coastal occupation from the Quinault River to the Columbia River, although the human population that existed there when the first Euro-Americans arrived was estimated at four thousand to six thousand. The beginning of an answer to the puzzle came in the 1980s, when geologists studying the tidal banks of Oregon's Salmon River found fire-cracked-rock hearths covered by a sheet of sand that had been laid down by a tsunami and by mud brought in by post-tsunami tides. These buried hearths became part of the case for recognizing the abrupt lowering of coastal land during an earthquake. Similar sand- and mud-covered human evidence was found along the tidal banks of Washington's Copalis River north of Grays Harbor, and at the Niawiakum River, an arm of Willapa Bay. Both of these sites have fragmented bones and shells lying among fire-cracked rocks. Such burial of archaeological sites by earthquakes may help explain why researchers found less evidence of prehistoric human populations along the Northwest Coast than would be expected—and the date of the earthquake now is known. It occurred in January 1700.

Making that determination involved "ghost forests" of still-standing bare red cedar trunks. They protrude through the tidal estuaries of the Copalis River and at Grays Harbor, Willapa Bay, and the Columbia River. Tidal water killed the trees when a land subsidence dropped their roots below high-tide level. Dating came from the outermost growth rings of cedar roots at all four locations, and the outer growth rings of nearby spruce stumps confirmed the date. The trees lived through the 1699 growing season but died suddenly before spring of the following year. The outer rings show little thinning, which would be expected if death had come gradually.

Remarkably, pinpointing an even more exact date for the earthquake was made possible by official village records in Japan. Scribes along six hundred miles of Pacific coastline there described a stupendous flooding that struck without known cause, drowning paddies, wrecking houses, and sinking boats. This occurred on January 27 and 28 (Japan time) in the year 1700. Nearly three centuries later—in 1996—a Japanese team of seismologists, an engineer, and a historian determined that the damage must have come from a tsunami that originated eight thousand miles away, on the Northwest Coast of North America. With its date and arrival hour in Japan documented, and knowing the jetliner speed of tsunamis crossing deep sea water, the team estimated that what is now known as the Cascadia Earthquake occurred on January 26, 1700, at 9 P.M. (Northwest time).

Maybe it was this shaking that triggered the mudflow that buried the houses at Ozette, both a human tragedy and the creation of a rich legacy—a legacy that is perhaps also laden with implications for present-day communities vulnerable to the effects of earthquakes and tsunamis.

A slit representing eyes continues around the head of this wooden carving, producing a face on both sides. The head measures five centimeters long; the carving's total length is forty-one centimeters.

Chapter Five

Legacy

THE IMPACT OF OZETTE

THE OZETTE STORY VERGES ON HYPERBOLE. "AS A NORTHWEST COAST archaeological site, it never has been equaled and probably never will be," according to Jim Hanson, training director for the Native American Museum Program of the Smithsonian Institution. "It is unique."

When the project began in 1966, little Northwest Coast archaeological research had been published. However, with the discovery of Ozette's remarkable preservation, that one site quickly gained widespread attention. Dr. Kenneth Ames, past president of the Society for American Archaeology, points out that Ozette is identified as exemplary in Colin Renfrew and Paul Bahn's *Archaeology: Theories, Methods and Practice* and is often the only Northwest Coast archaeology site mentioned in other textbooks and books for the general public. It is one of eleven sites for all of North America discussed by T. Douglas Price and Gary Feinman in their book *Images of the Past*, and one of eighteen (and the only North American West Coast site) in David H. Thomas's *Native North America*. Ames warns there seems to be a tendency toward what he calls "Ozetteopeia, an inability to see the rest of the coast," because of Ozette's immense scientific and cultural contributions.

In many ways Ozette archaeology confirmed Makah elders' memories and family traditions. It demonstrated the architecture of cedar-plank longhouses and the separate family areas within them. It also indicated what foods and raw materials were drawn upon and how the use of resources varied from one family to another and from house to house. The tools used to make other tools were present. So were artifacts in all stages of manufacture, use, and wear, and along with them were carvings that must have carried the spiritual and ritual power that belonged to

Archaeologists found artifacts, such as this comb, in all stages of manufacture. Unfinished objects facilitated understanding of the various activities within an individual house and from one house to another.

individual families or households. The uneven distribution of high-prestige items points toward the presence of social rank, and the whaling gear makes it clear that Ozette people actively hunted whales rather than just using dead whales that drifted ashore. A conspicuous abundance of food—more than could be immediately consumed—suggests knowledge of preserving and storing surplus for future use by villagers and for trade.

The Ozette legacy has affected our perception of not only Northwest Coast culture but also archaeology itself. The project drew on expertise from a variety of disciplines, and it greatly enhanced both scientific and public awareness of water-saturated sites and how to excavate them. At the project's major onset in the 1970s (preceded by two summers of preliminary work), there was essentially no precedent for a Native American tribe to instigate an archaeological investigation. Equally rare was an archaeologist's welcome of a tribe's participation. Fortunately, such partnerships are now becoming standard. Also ahead of its era was Professor Daugherty's belief that the public has a right to watch the excavation of a site, a conviction that led to daily tours for all who hiked the four miles from road's end to the site. Furthermore, Daugherty recognized the hunger of print and broadcast media for good stories, a situation stimulated by the recent availability of low-cost color printing and by television's increasing role in the presentation of information and entertainment. The beauty of

A hollow-bone or antler carving was probably a late-historic-period measure for gun powder.

Makah elders thought this bone carving lying in a broken mussel shell might represent Kwa-tii; his story tells that today's offshore islands came from the teeth of his comb.

Ozette's setting and the romance of operating a remote year-round research camp there heightened the project's appeal. So did the poignant drama of the catastrophic mudflow and the opportunity the site provided to compare historical and ethnographic reports with the actual record coming out of the ground.

In a sense, the Ozette project is ongoing. Archaeologists collected and preserved all that they uncovered—not just the showy artifacts but also the seemingly inconsequential, such as debris caught in the mesh of a water screen and wood chips from a craftsman's work bench, "signatures" of the tools that made them. Along with the tens of thousands of recovered objects and faunal remains are immense files of data and stratigraphic drawings. They provide opportunity to find answers to questions only beginning to be asked. Their evidence awaits questioning about topics unimagined when the excavation was in progress.

Even while excavation at Ozette was under way, Daugherty encouraged—and the tribe approved—investigation of other sites. Edward Friedman tested winter village and seasonal camp locations known historically and ethnographically. For eleven summers beginning in 1977, Dale Croes excavated at the mouth of the Hoko River, east of Neah Bay; discoveries include a rock shelter that had been occupied seasonally from about 1,000 to 100 years ago, fish camps 1,700 to 3,100 years old, and riverbank deposits holding cordage, baskets, mats, hats, a fishnet, and fishhooks 2,700 years old. Gary Wessen documented coastal occupation sites on the Makah Reservation that belong to a time when sea level stood five to fifteen meters above today's level, and when saltwater flooded the river valleys, Cape Flattery was an island, and beaches stretched where forests now flourish. The shorelines of this early landscape are now terraces well back from today's coastline, and on them is evidence of year-round human habitation as much as 4,000 years old. Wedges found there suggest woodworking skills possibly sufficient for producing house planks and canoes. Faunal remains indicate reliance on marine resources, including fur seals and whales—and this establishes the presence of seaworthy vessels and maritime skills millennia ago. Such archaeological investigations continue under contract with the Makah Tribal Historic Preservation Office, established in 2000 and operated as part of the Makah Cultural and Research Center.

Also, the Ozette collection, curated at the Makah Cultural and Research Center, continues to draw the attention of researchers. For example, Jonathan Scordino, biologist with Makah Fisheries Management, a tribal agency, led a study hoping to find why halibut hooks from Ozette selectively caught only halibut, as is known from oral history and ethnographic records, whereas today's commercial hooks intended for halibut also produce an undesirable bycatch of rockfish, dogfish, and others. So far, test results suggest replicated Ozette hooks may not solve the commercial problem but do show promise for sports fishing. Liz Alter, a University of California graduate student, studied the whale bones from Ozette and the older sites identified by Dr. Wessen, as part of her research on whale population dynamics with a focus on DNA identification rather than bone morphology. For Mike Etnier, a University of Washington graduate student, research focused on fur seal bones and teeth from Ozette, which he hoped might help identify former rookery locations. Access to the collection for all such studies is subject to approval by the trustees of the Makah Cultural and Research Center.

BRIDGING TIME

"Ozette has inspired a lot of people here to look into our heritage," points out Greig Arnold, who was, in 1979, the first director of the Makah Cultural and Research Center. "It's brought young people close to senior citizens."

For the Makahs, discoveries at Ozette reaffirmed aspects of culture. Their impact helped reverse long years of government misunderstanding and opposition to inherent values. More than twenty young Makahs worked at the excavation site and in the laboratory. Through archaeology they helped discover and preserve part of their cultural past and, at the same time, were exposed to science as a methodology and way of thinking. No road reached Neah Bay until the 1930s. Even then the community

Voices

Our children should know where we came from. These [Ozette] things . . . prove our heritage, which our older people, so many generations, have told us about.

— LUKE MARKISHTUM, Makah senior citizen in a 1978 interview

Makah elders often visited the Neah Bay laboratory to see what the helicopter had brought from the excavations at Ozette. *Shown here:* Helen Peterson *(left)*, Harold Ides, Meredith (Phillips) Parker.

Well, at least to me, Ozette showed me who I really am, and It proved once again that we have been here for a good long time. We aren't "imports."

— HILARY IRVING, Makah senior citizen in a 1978 interview

The Ozette artifacts give a lot of pride and a real orientation to *our* culture. . . . My high school daughter worked at the museum as a tour guide, and she came home saying, "I didn't realize what a background I have."

— MARY LOU DENNY, Makah schoolteacher in a 1979 interview

Look at the technology they had then. . . . They even carved figures into [things] of practical, everyday use. When you carve a piece like that and give it form, it is like you are giving it life. It's no longer just an object. It's more.

— LANCE WILKE, Makah carver and archaeology crew member at Ozette

My grandma lived at Ozette, . . . and one time she said they were short of men to go whaling. Well, they asked Grandma to go along, so she went. And they did catch a whale that time. My, she said, she was so afraid when the whale came up beside them.

—Isabell Ides, Makah senior citizen in a 1978 interview

Everybody was all the time going places in canoes then. They were big. . . . They could carry three families at once. We used to go to Victoria after the last of the halibut was dried—six or seven canoes of us. We children were different then. We knew how to sit still. We would leave at nine in the morning and get to Victoria at five that same day. Grandmother and the other ladies took big bags with the baskets they had made, and they went to Hudson's Bay [Company] and traded for cloth and shawls.

—Ada Markishtum, Makah senior citizen in an interview circa 1960

Ozette artifacts . . . give credence to what the old people were saying. . . . I'd talk with my grandfather, and he'd tell me something ten times and it was always the same. Oral history was accurate, but now we can see concretely what [our grandparents] were talking about. They were told to forget everything, and now we're trying to get it back. To find out who we are.

—Ron Johnson, Makah teacher and basketball coach in a 1978 interview

To make the Indian comply with European principles of social behavior, it became necessary to separate him from his own values and disengage him from his natural tendencies of pluralism. . . . Democracy advocates a respect and concern for individualism as a birthright. Tribal approaches are more of a self-sacrifice, a self-fulfillment with close relationships with family and community.

—Lloyd Colfax, Makah director of Native Studies at Evergreen State College, Olympia, in a 1978 interview

The Ozette project started, and I think maybe the awareness of our culture has bloomed a little more.

—Kathy Ides Flinn, Makah conservator for Ozette artifacts

They must have been awful damn tough. No shoes. Look at what the weather is like out here. You would have thought they'd all die of pneumonia.

—Lance Wilke, Makah carver and archaeology crew member at Ozette

Makah high school and college students joined the Ozette project. *Shown here,* Meredith Parker cleaning a basket at the excavation site; Mike Bowechop excavating a box; and Debbie Cook working in the Neah Bay laboratory.

had remained isolated, a place where men returning home from World War II military service resumed fishing from dugout canoes, and where women never stopped weaving baskets, telling Makah stories to children, and teaching them dances for the annual Makah Days celebration of attaining citizenship. The American Stars and Stripes had first been raised at Neah Bay in 1913, by the third Wanamaker Expedition which was presenting flags to many tribes across the nation and inviting them to sign a "Declaration of Allegiance" to the United States. This was in anticipation of the 1924 American Indian Citizenship Act which (finally!) made citizens of all Indians born in the United States.

Archaeologist Daugherty recalled mentioning to the Makah Tribal Council at the outset of the Ozette project that "the material coming out of the ground will need a lot of care over the years, and that will mean a first-class facility." The immediate reaction was: "All right. We'll have one." It was a concept far from traditional. Sharing ownership of the Ozette artifacts runs counter to family ownership. As Arnold expresses it: "Traditionally, nothing was owned by everybody. It was *somebody's* stuff. And that's just the way it was."

One of the challenges of developing a "first-class facility" was to bridge the ownership disparity by somehow linking cultural traits with modern museum management. A grant from the National Endowment for the Arts made it possible for Makah students to take classes in museology at the University of Washington and the Burke Museum in Seattle. The federal Economic Development Administration funded a museum and culture center, recognizing its potential to stimulate tourism and to provide a sales outlet for Makah artists and craftspeople. To work with a Makah planning committee on exhibit design, Dr. Daugherty contacted Jean Andre, at the time on furlough from his position as head designer for the British Columbia Provincial Museum (now the Royal British Columbia Museum) and widely known for his sensitivity in working with the people represented by the exhibits. The provincial museum's location in Victoria, a few miles across the Strait of Juan de Fuca from Neah Bay, make it virtually a Neah Bay neighbor, and its exhibits of Canada's First Nations culture fit well with Makah culture.

To aid their focus, the committee and Andre spent several days at Ozette seeing the excavation at firsthand, walking the beach, hearing the surf, watching whales spout, and listening to the gulls and the eagles. They concluded that the museum should do more than merely display objects. It should present them in a context that would create a bridge from the time of the Ozette ancestors to the present. Furthermore, the tribe had decided that the museum was not to stand alone. It would be part of a Makah Cultural and Research Center.

The result is a complex of buildings standing at the base of the hill sloping down to the curve of the Neah Bay beach. In the museum, about fifteen thousand visitors a year enter a full-scale replica of an Ozette house, handle the paddles and bailers and mats of replicated canoes, and view the actual artifacts from Ozette—the harpoons and hooks, the baskets and boxes, the wall panel with thunderbirds and wolves and the whale-fin effigy inlaid with seven hundred sea otter teeth, as well as the tools that created all these and more. They see the skeleton of the gray whale successfully hunted in 1999, its bones cleaned and rearticulated by Makah high school students. The skeleton's presence in the museum exemplifies Makah ability to integrate treaty rights and ongoing cultural importance with that of the Ozette past. As Makah artist Greg Colfax has written for the entry gallery:

The Ozette houses are canoes carrying scientists into a world that respects the oral history of our people. The Ozette houses are war clubs against ignorance and hostility. The Ozette houses are thunder and lightning for Makahs, voices from the past illuminating our heritage. At Ozette, endings have become beginnings. From Ozette comes new understanding.

Makah museology students made a cedar dugout canoe and tested it in the Strait of Juan de Fuca.

Collections management embraces this dual sensitivity. It is computerized but also safeguards traditions. For example, Makah elder Helma Ward, a member of the four-person collections management committee, remembers gender-specific restrictions that prohibit women from touching harpoon blades or fishhooks. This translates into the museum staff women being allowed to lift trays holding such artifacts but not to rearrange the individual items. Similarly, linguistics can affect collections policies. What to English speakers are diverse objects may be categorized very differently in Makah. Thus, the Makah words for canoe paddles, wedges, chisels, adzes, and metal all end with the same suffix, *yak*, which means "thing that you use to perform a certain action." Use is definitive, and in use these objects are all held perpendicular to the surface they work on. Metal is included in this category because it can be made into a blade that will be held perpendicular while in use.

The museum opened in 1979. Its exhibits of the legacy retrieved from Ozette were designed to "speak" to both the public and the tribe. Additionally, an oral history program safeguards recorded interviews, holding them with due regard for family restrictions on their use. Photographs are similarly archived, as are ethnographic and historical documents. A Makah dictionary has been compiled using a variation of the International Phonetic Alphabet; signs on village buildings are in Makah; gro-

An exquisite Ozette wooden carving is thought by some to be an owl, by others to be an octopus. The head measures fourteen by eleven centimeters; the whole carving, which has two small heads at the base, measures forty-five centimeters long.

LEGACY

cery store shelves have been labeled in Makah; a quarterly newsletter is printed in Makah; and sports enthusiasts cheer victory in Makah. The language is now the official language of Neah Bay, including new words to express new realities. Computers are "things that think."

Greig Arnold likens Makah culture to sand in an hourglass. Gone are the elders who remembered the last cedar longhouses and living at Ozette, who knew the taste of fresh whale oil on dried fish, and who had their mouths washed out with soap for speaking Makah at boarding school. "We're at the very end of our hourglass from the real old times," Arnold says. "We're pulling the last of the sand through. And whatever it is that we get, when the last Makah speaker is gone, we then turn [the hourglass] over and start again."

Excavating the whaling village at Ozette came at a pivotal time.

ILLUSTRATION CREDITS

Photographs by Ruth Kirk except as noted here.

Archaeology camp, lower left photo (page 25): Mary Randlett

Replica house (page 28), carving of whale (page 35), and metal tool (page 46): Gary Wessen

Carving of whale fin inlaid with otter teeth (page 32), seal clubs (page 63), four baskets (page 67), and box front (page 72): Ozette Project, photos by Mike Short

Fire (page 58): Paul Gleeson

Seals (page 63): Alaska Fisheries Science Center, NOAA Fisheries Service, photo by Rolf Ream

Whale (page 49): Alaska Fisheries Science Center, NOAA Fisheries Service, photo by Merrill Gosho

Thunderbird and wolves panel (page 35): drawing by Dale Croes

Basket (page 15), whaler's pouch (page 47), cedar-bough withe (page 65), cedar-bough rope (page 65), pack basket (page 67), house (page 73): Ozette Project, drawings by Chris Walsh

INDEX

A

abraders, 71

acetone, 58

A day ah tha wa, x

advanced degrees. *See* dissertations; master's theses

Advisory Council on Historic Preservation, 42

adzes, 64, 71

Ahlstrom, Lars (homesteader), xiv

albatross bone, 63

alder, 70

alpacas, 45

Alter, Liz (researcher), 84

American Indian Citizenship Act, 87

Americans: Northwest Coast cultures' contacts with Euro-Americans, 5–6, 22, 26, 46, 46*fig.*, 87

Ames, Kenneth (archaeologist), 81

Andre, Jean (museum exhibit designer), 88

animal husbandry, 45

animal remains. *See* fauna and faunal remains; *specific animals*

Arnold, Greig (first director of Makah Cultural and Reseach Center), 84, 91

arrows and arrow points, 29, 45, 57, 66, 70

artifacts. *See* Ozette artifacts

Austria shipwreck, 14

awls, 31, 63, 67

B

bark beaters, 64

Barker, Nora (Makah elder), 37, 37*fig.*

bark objects. *See* cordage and basketry; fiber and fiber objects

bark shredders, 64

barnacles, 47, 48*fig.*

baskets, 15*fig.*, 16*figs.*, 66–67, 66*fig.*, 67*figs. See also* cordage and basketry

battens, 45, 45*fig.*

bears, 33, 61

beavers and beaver teeth, 61, 71, 71*fig.*; beaver-tooth dice, 39, 40*fig.*

benches and bench planks, 29, 44, 47, 74, 75

Biederbost wet site, 15

bird bones, 31, 60, 62–63

blades, 31, 46, 46*fig.*, 47, 48*fig.*, 62, 64, 71–72

blankets, 30–31, 45, 63

blue whale, 64

bogs, 15

Boldt, George H. (judge), 57, 58

bone objects, 8, 29, 31, 62–63, 64–65, 71; carvings, 83*figs.*; combs, 8, 9*fig.*, 33*fig.*, 40*figs. See also* fauna and faunal remains; *other specific types of objects*

Bowechop, Mike (Ozette crew member), 87*fig.*

bowls, 15, 39, 41*fig.*, 42, 57, 71

bows, 29, 57, 66, 70

Ozette excavation (*cont.*)
significance for the Makah, xii, 20–21, 81–82, 84–91; site characteristics, xiii–xiv, 3, 5–7; supply and communications logistics, 21, 24, 24*fig.*, 30, 33–34, 43, 43*fig.*; Tribal Council support for, 4, 19, 20–21, 30, 82; tribe members' participation, x–xi, xii, 30, 39, 58, 84, 87*figs.*; volunteer participation, 42–43; work methods, 8, 10–11, 26–27. *See also* houses; Ozette artifacts; Ozette Field Laboratory

Ozette Field Laboratory (Neah Bay), 21, 36, 39–42, 58; tribe members as staff and visitors, xi, xii, xiv, 58, 85*fig.*, 87*fig.*

Ozette village: abandonment of, 3, 37; Makah's ties to, x, xiv, 37; resource availability, 6–7, 33–34, 82; site of, 2*fig.*, 3, 5–7; U.S. recognition of tribal land ownership, 37

P

paddles. *See* canoe paddles

paint pigments, 67

Parker, Meredith, ix–xii, 87*fig.*

Parker, Meredith Phillips (grandmother of Meredith Parker), ix–x, xi, 85*fig.*

Parker, Paul, Sr., (grandfather of Meredith Parker), ix

Parker, Theron (member of 1999 whaling crew), 51

Parker. Ty (Makah tribal member), 73

Parker, Wilson (whaler and great grandfather of Meridith Parker), x

pelican bone, 63

Penn, Bill (Quileute elder), 66

Peterson, Helen (Makah elder), 37, 85*fig.*

plants and soils, xiv, 7–8; midden core samples, 11, 12. *See also* fiber; forests; middens; wood; *specific plants and woods*

polyethylene glycol (Carbowax), 40, 41, 58

porpoise bones, 63

posts, postholes, and support posts, 11, 13, 24, 27, 47, 53, 56, 57, 67, 73, 74, 74*fig.*, 75, 78

pumps, 26, 27

Q

Queen Charlotte Islands (archaeological sites), 15

R

radioactive-carbon dating, 76–77

Reagan, Albert (early coastal archaeological survey), 19

resource availability, 6–7, 22, 33–34, 82

Rice, Harvey (graduate student), 12, 26

right whale, 64

river otter, 61

roofs, 3, 19, 35, 44, 47, 73, 74

rope, 65–66, 65*fig. See also* cordage and basketry

rosin, 58

Royal British Columbia Museum, 88

S

Salish baskets, 67*fig.*

salmon and salmon fishing, 22, 57–58; salmon roasting sticks, 70–71, 71*fig.*

Salmon River (Oregon), 79

Scordino, Jonathan (Makah Fisheries biologist), 84

sea lions, 7*fig.*, 63

seals and seal bones, 6–7, 8, 13, 22, 55, 63*fig.*; hunting and consumption of, 10, 62–64; feast dish with seal carving, 53; remains found, 10, 11, 13, 55, 63–64; seal hunting and hunting tools, 10, 20, 45, 62–63, 63*figs.*, 70, 84; seal oil, 42, 47

sea otter and sea otter remains, 22, 64; whale fin carving set with sea otter teeth, 31, 32*fig.*, 33*fig.*

shells, 47, 60, 62; mussel-shell points and blades, 47, 48*fig.*, 71–72; snail opercula, 31, 47

shipwrecks, 5, 14

shoes. *See* mudshoes

skunks, 61

slavery, 23, 67